Enrich Book

Grade

GO MATH!

PROVIDES Daily Enrichment Activities

HOUGHTON MIFFLIN HARCOURT

Copyright © by Houghton Mifflin Harcourt Publishing Company.

All rights reserved. No part of this work may be reproduced or transmitted in any form or by any means, electronic or mechanical, including photocopying or recording, or by any information storage and retrieval system, without the prior written permission of the copyright owner unless such copying is expressly permitted by federal copyright law. Requests for permission to make copies of any part of the work should be addressed to Houghton Mifflin Harcourt Publishing Company, Attn: Contracts, Copyrights, and Licensing, 9400 South Park Center Loop, Orlando, Florida 32819.

Printed in the U.S.A.

ISBN 978-0-547-58818-6

2 3 4 5 6 7 8 9 10   0982   20 19 18 17 16 15 14 13 12 11

4500319270   B C D E F G

If you have received these materials as examination copies free of charge, Houghton Mifflin Harcourt Publishing Company retains title to the materials and they may not be resold. Resale of examination copies is strictly prohibited.

Possession of this publication in print format does not entitle users to convert this publication, or any portion of it, into electronic format.

Table of Contents

CRITICAL AREA: Place Value and Operations with Whole Numbers

Chapter 1: Place Value, Addition, and Subtraction to One Million

1.1	Comparing Values	E1
1.2	Period Posers	E2
1.3	Place-Value Puzzle	E3
1.4	Rounding Ranges	E4
1.5	Number Comparisons	E5
1.6	3-Foot Path	E6
1.7	Unknown Digits	E7
1.8	Take a Seat!	E8

Chapter 2: Multiply by 1-Digit Numbers

2.1	Multiplication Match-Up	E9
2.2	Mixed Models	E10
2.3	Multiplication Inequalities	E11
2.4	Find the Unknown Factors	E12
2.5	Shading the Grids	E13
2.6	Expanded Form Match-Up	E14
2.7	Shaping Factors	E15
2.8	Multiply by 11 Mentally	E16
2.9	2-Digit Roses	E17
2.10	Regrouping Review	E18
2.11	Multiplication Mystery	E19
2.12	Same Answer Multistep	E20

Chapter 3: Multiply 2-Digit Numbers

3.1	Multiplying with Tens	E21
3.2	Decode the Message	E22
3.3	The Lattice Method	E23
3.4	Reverse and Record	E24
3.5	Multiplication Mystery	E25
3.6	Product Pairs	E26
3.7	Pastry Chef's Problem	E27

Chapter 4: Divide by 1-Digit Numbers

4.1	Estimating Quotients	E28
4.2	Riddle Time	E29
4.3	Remainder Jeopardy	E30
4.4	Dividend Riddles	E31
4.5	Make the Best Estimate	E32
4.6	True or Not True?	E33
4.7	Subtraction Situations	E34
4.8	Special Delivery	E35
4.9	Division Drying	E36
4.10	How Many Digits?	E37
4.11	What Is Left Over?	E38
4.12	It's a Riddle!	E39

Chapter 5: Factors, Multiples, and Patterns

5.1	Festive Factors	E40
5.2	Invisible Divisible	E41
5.3	Common Ground	E42
5.4	Multiple Dates	E43
5.5	Prime Search	E44
5.6	Pattern Perfect	E45

CRITICAL AREA: Fractions and Decimals

Chapter 6: Fraction Equivalence and Comparison

6.1	Equivalent Fraction Find	E46
6.2	Equivalent Art	E47
6.3	To Simplify or Not To Simplify?	E48
6.4	Common Denominator Combos	E49
6.5	Factors, Fractions, and Fruit	E50
6.6	At the Pet Store	E51
6.7	Parts of a Project	E52
6.8	Filling Cups	E53

Chapter 7: Add and Subtract Fractions

7.1	Fraction Fun	E54
7.2	Mixed-Up Sums	E55
7.3	Sum Fractions!	E56
7.4	Fraction Food	E57
7.5	Fraction Equations	E58
7.6	The Rename Game	E59
7.7	Finding Mixed Numbers	E60
7.8	Leftovers	E61
7.9	Mixing Properties	E62
7.10	Problem Solving with Fractions	E63

Chapter 8: Multiply Fractions by Whole Numbers

- 8.1 Mixed Numbers and Unit Fractions ... E64
- 8.2 Multiples of Mixed Numbers ... E65
- 8.3 Fraction of a Whole Number ... E66
- 8.4 Unknown Numbers ... E67
- 8.5 Heights and Depths ... E68

Chapter 9: Relate Fractions and Decimals

- 9.1 Model, Decimal, and Fraction ... E69
- 9.2 Which Hundredth Is It? ... E70
- 9.3 Matching Fractions and Decimals ... E71
- 9.4 Money Matters ... E72
- 9.5 School Store ... E73
- 9.6 Adding Fractions and Decimals ... E74
- 9.7 Comparing Decimals ... E75

CRITICAL AREA: Geometry, Measurement, and Data

Chapter 10: Two-Dimensional Figures

10.1	Line Art	E76
10.2	Triangle Living	E77
10.3	Alphabet Soup	E78
10.4	Quad Logic	E79
10.5	Swimming Pool Symmetry	E80
10.6	Symmetry Riddle	E81
10.7	Pentomino Patterns	E82

Chapter 11: Angles

11.1	A Turning Riddle	E83
11.2	Time by Degrees	E84
11.3	Drawing Triangles	E85
11.4	Degrees of Separation	E86
11.5	Unknown Measures	E87

Chapter 12: Relative Sizes of Measurement Units

- 12.1 Estimation Match-Up ... E88
- 12.2 Inching Closer ... E89
- 12.3 Weighty Matters ... E90
- 12.4 Using Measures of Liquid Volume ... E91
- 12.5 Discover the Line Plot ... E92
- 12.6 Going to Greater Lengths ... E93
- 12.7 More Volume, Less Mass ... E94
- 12.8 Passing the Time ... E95
- 12.9 Do You Have the Time? ... E96
- 12.10 Mixed Measures ... E97
- 12.11 Two-Step Patterns ... E98

Chapter 13: Algebra: Perimeter and Area

- 13.1 Perimeter Puzzlers ... E99
- 13.2 Aiden's Garden ... E100
- 13.3 Unusual Measures ... E101
- 13.4 Rectangular Riddles ... E102
- 13.5 Building Bedrooms ... E103

Name _____

Lesson 1.1
Enrich

Comparing Values

Compare the values of the underlined digits.

1. 3,<u>4</u>92 and 70<u>4</u>

   The value of 4 in _____

   is _____ times

   the value of 4 in _____.

2. <u>8</u>,596 and 9<u>8</u>5

   The value of 8 in _____

   is _____ times

   the value of 8 in _____.

3. <u>2</u>,481 and 5,07<u>2</u>

   The value of 2 in _____

   is _____ times

   the value of 2 in _____.

4. 4<u>3</u>,158 and 71,4<u>3</u>5

   The value of 3 in _____

   is _____ times

   the value of 3 in _____.

5. 4<u>9</u>5,123 and 63,12<u>9</u>

   The value of 9 in _____

   is _____ times

   the value of 9 in _____.

6. <u>5</u>06,712 and 324,8<u>5</u>9

   The value of 5 in _____

   is _____ times

   the value of 5 in _____.

7. <u>8</u>37,164 and 4,50<u>8</u>

   The value of 8 in _____

   is _____ times

   the value of 8 in _____.

8. <u>6</u>31,485 and <u>6</u>82

   The value of 6 in _____

   is _____ times

   the value of 6 in _____.

9. **Stretch Your Thinking** Write a pair of numbers such that the value of the 7 in the first number is 1,000 times the value of the 7 in the second number, and the value of the 3 in the first number is 100 times the value of the 3 in the second number.

_____

Enrich   E1   Grade 4
© Houghton Mifflin Harcourt Publishing Company

Name _____

Lesson 1.2
Enrich

Period Posers

Solve each riddle.

1. **Fred:** My number has two periods. One period contains the digits 3, 0, and 6 in that order. The other contains the digits 0, 9, and 5 in that order.

   Ned: My number has two periods also. One contains the digits 4, 8, and 6 in that order. The other period contains the digits 1, 2, and 7 in that order.

   Fred: Yes, but my number is greater than your number.

   What are Fred's and Ned's numbers?

   _____

   _____

2. **Ann:** My number has two periods. One contains the digits 4, 1, and 8 in that order. The other contains the digit 9.

   Jan: My number has two periods. One period contains only 0s. The other has the digits 1 and 0 in that order.

   Ann: Too bad, my number must be greater than your number.

   Jan: Nope—my number is greater!

   What are Ann's and Jan's numbers?

   _____

   _____

3. **Mo:** My number has two periods. One period has a 7 in the hundreds place. The other has an 8 in the tens place.

   Bo: My number also has two periods. One has a 1 in the hundreds place. The other has a 2 in the tens place.

   Mo: All other digits in our numbers are zeros. So how can it be that your number is greater than my number?

   What are Mo's and Bo's numbers?

   _____

4. **Stretch Your Thinking** Write your own period poser. Then exchange it with a classmate and solve each other's posers.

   _____

   _____

Name _____

Lesson 1.3
Enrich

Place-Value Puzzle

Fill in each blank with a digit that will make the number sentence true. The digits to choose from are listed in the box under each number sentence. Use each digit only once.

1. 1 __ 5,120 > 125, __ 20 > 125,1 __ 0

   | 1, 2, 3 |

2. 4 __ 3,900 < 42 __ ,900 = 423, __ 00 < 42 __ ,900

   | 1, 3, 4, 9 |

3. 27 __ ,010 < 2 __ 8,010 < 29 __ ,010

   | 7, 8, 9 |

4. 3 __ ,788 > 35,7 __ 8 = 35, __ 88 > 35, __ 88

   | 5, 6, 7, 8 |

5. 6 __ 8,138 > 6 __ 7,294 < 63 __ ,705

   | 3, 4, 9 |

6. 4 __ 6,047 > __ 63,941 = 463, __ 41 > __ 86, __ 42

   | 3, 4, 5, 7, 9 |

7. 101,5 __ 2 > 1 __ 1,508 > 101, __ 62 > 101,3 __ 7

   | 0, 3, 5, 8 |

8. **Write Math** If you know A is greater than B and B is greater than C, do you have to compare A to C to know which is greater? Use an example to explain.

_____

_____

Enrich   E3   Grade 4
© Houghton Mifflin Harcourt Publishing Company

Name _____

Lesson 1.4
Enrich

Rounding Ranges

Solve each riddle. Give your answer as a range of numbers.

1. When rounded to the nearest hundred, I become 500. What numbers could I be?

   _____

2. When rounded to the nearest ten, I become 500. What numbers could I be?

   _____

3. When rounded to the nearest thousand, I become 3,000. What numbers could I be?

   _____

4. When rounded to the nearest hundred, I become 3,000. What numbers could I be?

   _____

5. When rounded to the nearest hundred thousand, I become 600,000. What numbers could I be?

   _____

6. When rounded to the nearest ten thousand, I become 600,000. What numbers could I be?

   _____

7. **Write Math** ▶ Compare the ranges of your answers to Exercises 2, 4, and 6 to the ranges in Exercises 1, 3, and 5. What do you notice? Give a reason for your observation.

   _____
   _____
   _____
   _____

Enrich
E4
Grade 4
© Houghton Mifflin Harcourt Publishing Company

Name _____

Lesson 1.5
Enrich

Number Comparisons

Compare the numbers. Write <, >, or =.

1. 400 tens ◯ 48 hundreds

2. 7 thousands, 8 hundreds ◯ 2,500 tens

3. 715 thousands, 34 tens ◯ 715,034

4. 10 thousands, 5 hundreds ◯ 1,050 tens

5. 34 ten thousands, 85 hundreds ◯ 348,500

6. 6 hundred thousands, 47 tens ◯ 60 ten thousands, 4 hundreds

7. 2 ten thousands, 45 hundreds ◯ 308 hundreds

8. 25 thousands, 56 ones ◯ 3 ten thousands, 17 hundreds

9. 476 thousands ◯ 4 hundred thousands, 76 hundreds

10. 35 ten thousands, 8 hundreds ◯ 3 hundred thousands 50 thousands, 80 tens

11. **Write Math** ▸ Look back at Exercise 5. **Explain** how you found the answer.

_____
_____
_____
_____

Enrich   E5   Grade 4
© Houghton Mifflin Harcourt Publishing Company

Lesson 1.6
Enrich

Name _____

3-Foot Path

Find the path with the addends that correctly lead from the START box to the FIRST SUM box, and from there to the sum in the FINISH box. Then write the letters of the 5 boxes on your path in order to answer the riddle.

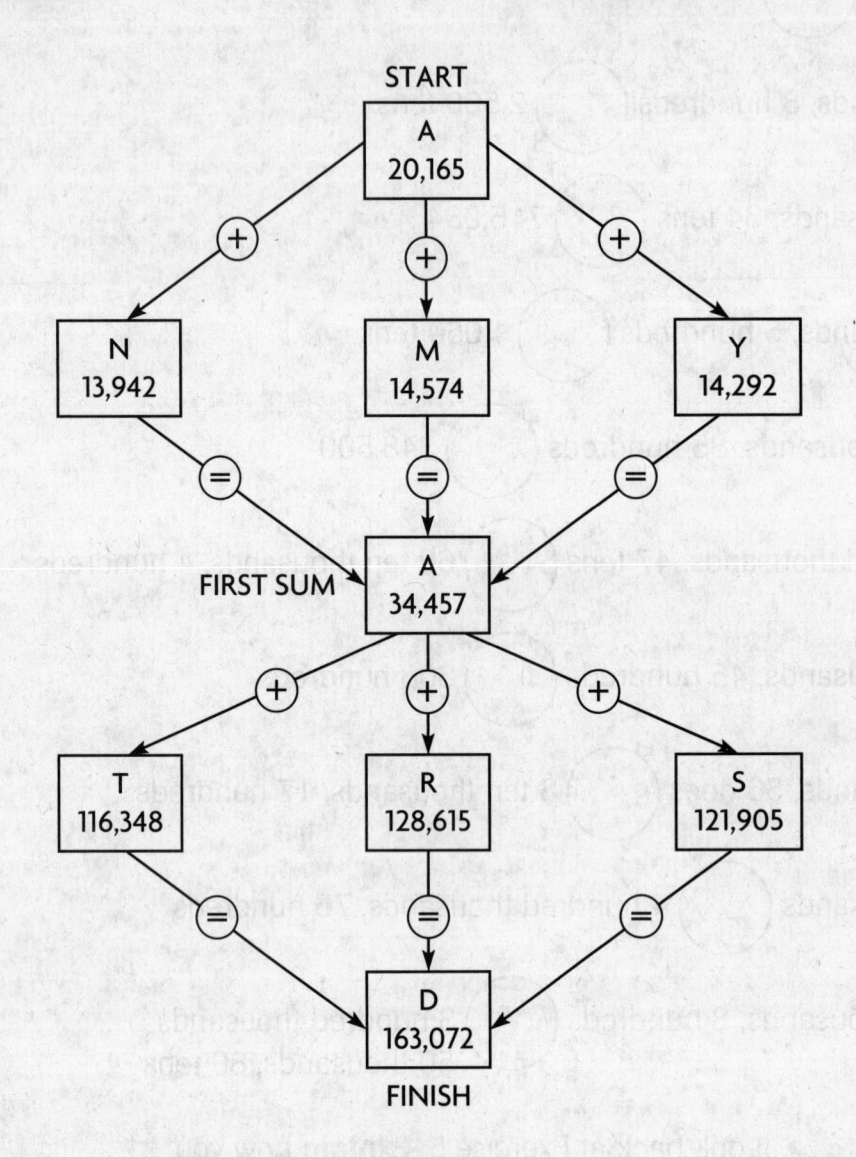

START
A
20,165

N 13,942   M 14,574   Y 14,292

FIRST SUM
A
34,457

T 116,348   R 128,615   S 121,905

D
163,072
FINISH

Where can you buy a ruler that is 3 feet long?

AT A   Y A R D SALE

Enrich   E6   Grade 4
© Houghton Mifflin Harcourt Publishing Company

Name _____

Lesson 1.7
Enrich

Unknown Digits

Complete each subtraction problem by finding the unknown digits.

1.
```
   4 2,☐ 5 3
 − 2 ☐, 3 4 ☐
 ─────────────
   1 5, 2 ☐ 6
```

2.
```
   9 0, 7 ☐ ☐
 − ☐ 3, ☐ 9 5
 ─────────────
   4 ☐, 9 3 6
```

3.
```
   ☐ 4 1, ☐ 1 ☐
 − 1 2 8, 7 ☐ 1
 ───────────────
   1 ☐ ☐, 8 9 7
```

4.
```
   6 3 ☐, ☐ ☐ 2
 − ☐ ☐ 5, 6 3 ☐
 ───────────────
   4 5 4, 8 0 8
```

5.
```
   ☐ 0 ☐, 3 ☐ 7
 −       8, 7 5 ☐
 ───────────────
   ☐ 7, ☐ 6 8
```

6.
```
   ☐ 0 0, ☐ ☐ ☐
 − 2 3 8, 1 7 2
 ───────────────
   4 ☐ ☐, 8 2 8
```

7. **Write Math** ▶ Describe what strategy you used to complete the unknown-digit subtraction problems. Use an example to explain.

_____
_____
_____
_____
_____
_____
_____
_____

Name _____

Lesson 1.8
Enrich

Take a Seat!

Use the table for 1–5.

1. Last night's game at the arena in Cleveland was 251 seats short of being filled to capacity. How many people attended the game?

   _____

Basketball Arena Seating Capacities	
City	**Capacity**
Cleveland	20,562
Boston	18,624
Atlanta	20,300
New Orleans	18,500
Los Angeles	18,997

2. How many more people can be seated in the largest arena than can be seated in the smallest arena?

   _____

3. Estimate the difference in the seating capacities of the Atlanta and Los Angeles arenas. **Explain** how you made your estimate.

   _____

   _____

4. There are two sold-out basketball games tonight. One is at the arena in Boston, and the other is at the arena in New Orleans. How many people are attending the two games?

   _____

5. **Write Math** The biggest college basketball arena seats 33,000. Is the combined capacity of the Cleveland and Boston arenas greater than or less than the capacity of the biggest college arena? How much greater or less? **Explain**.

   _____

   _____

   _____

Enrich E8 Grade 4
© Houghton Mifflin Harcourt Publishing Company

Name _____

Lesson 2.1
Enrich

Multiplication Match-Up

Match each word problem to a model. Write the equation and solve.

1. Angie has 36 coins. This is 4 times as many coins as Scott has. How many coins does Scott have?

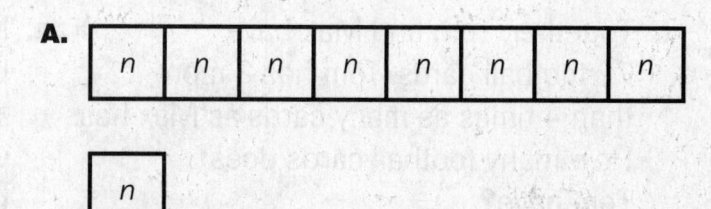

   _____

   A. | n | n | n | n | n | n | n | n |

   | n |

2. Yoshi bought 20 stamps. This is 5 times the number of postcards that Yoshi bought. How many postcards did Yoshi buy?

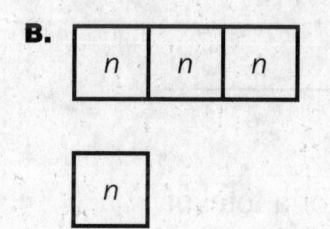

   _____

   B. | n | n | n |

   | n |

3. Jessica has 48 stickers. This is 8 times as many stickers as Taylor has. How many stickers does Taylor have?

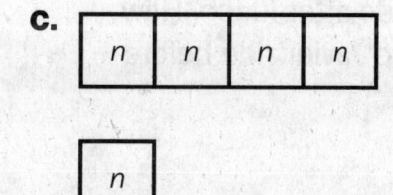

   _____

   C. | n | n | n | n |

   | n |

4. Joshua picked 24 apples. This is 3 times the number of apples that Carly picked. How many apples did Carly pick?

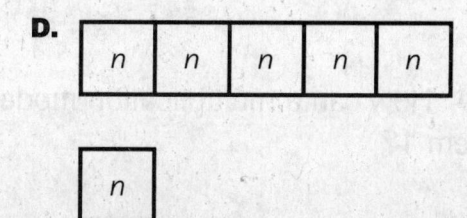

   _____

   D. | n | n | n | n | n |

   | n |

5. **Stretch Your Thinking** Write four comparison sentences for the product 12.

   _____

   _____

Enrich   E9   Grade 4

Name _____

Lesson 2.2
Enrich

Mixed Models

Solve each problem.

1. Together, Tom and Max have 72 football cards. Tom has 2 more than 4 times as many cards as Max has. How many football cards does Tom have?

   _____

2. Naomi has 50 red beads and white beads. The number of red beads is 1 more than 6 times the number of white beads. How many red beads does Naomi have?

   _____

3. Javier rode his bike for a total of 41 minutes. Before lunch, he rode for 1 minute less than 5 times the number of minutes he rode after lunch. How many minutes did Javier ride before lunch?

   _____

4. Marnie practiced her basketball dribbling. After two tries, she had bounced the ball 88 times. On the second try, she had 2 fewer bounces than 8 times the number of bounces she had on the first try. How many bounces did she have on the second try?

   _____

5. **Write Math** How can a multiplication model help you solve Problem 1?

   _____
   _____
   _____
   _____

Enrich
E10
Grade 4

© Houghton Mifflin Harcourt Publishing Company

Name _____

Lesson 2.3
Enrich

Multiplication Inequalities

Write <, >, or = for each ◯.

1. 7 × 60 ◯ 400
2. 700 ◯ 90 × 8
3. 3 × 800 ◯ 2,500
4. 2,000 ◯ 400 × 5
5. 8 × 6,000 ◯ 40,000
6. 3 × 9,000 ◯ 39,000
7. 6 × 900 ◯ 700 × 8
8. 8 × 3,000 ◯ 6,000 × 4
9. 9 × 4,000 ◯ 6,000 × 6
10. 800 × 9 ◯ 3,000 × 3

11. **Write Math** **Explain** how you found the answer in Exercise 10.

_____

_____

_____

_____

Enrich
E11
Grade 4
© Houghton Mifflin Harcourt Publishing Company

Name _____

Lesson 2.4
Enrich

Find the Unknown Factors

Choose two factors from the box to make the estimated product.
You may use the factors more than once.

3	5	624
9	126	957

1. 1,800 _____ × _____
2. 500 _____ × _____
3. 5,000 _____ × _____
4. 900 _____ × _____

8	7	435
6	899	273

5. 1,800 _____ × _____
6. 6,300 _____ × _____
7. 3,200 _____ × _____
8. 2,100 _____ × _____

5	6,149	3,044
2	3	8,756

9. 30,000 _____ × _____
10. 6,000 _____ × _____
11. 9,000 _____ × _____
12. 45,000 _____ × _____

13. **Stretch Your Thinking** Two factors have an estimated product of 10,000. One of these factors is a single digit. What two factors could they be? **Explain** your thinking.

_____

_____

_____

_____

Name _____

Lesson 2.5
Enrich

Shading the Grids

Use the Distributive Property. Shade and label each grid.

1. Show 3 × 28 in two different ways.

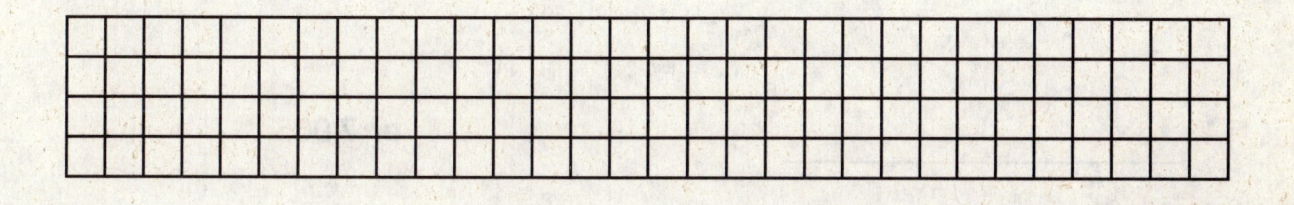

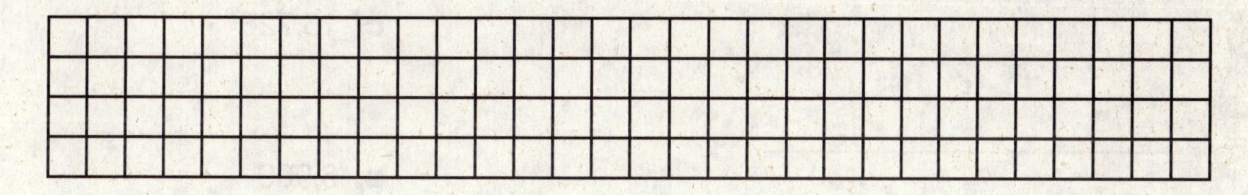

2. Show 4 × 23 in two different ways.

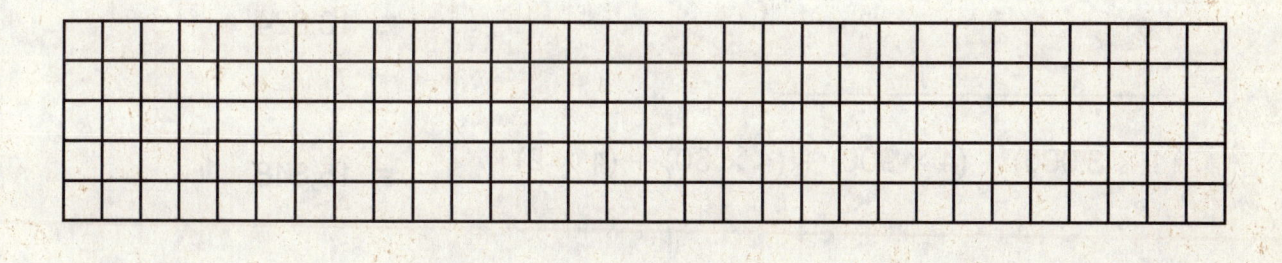

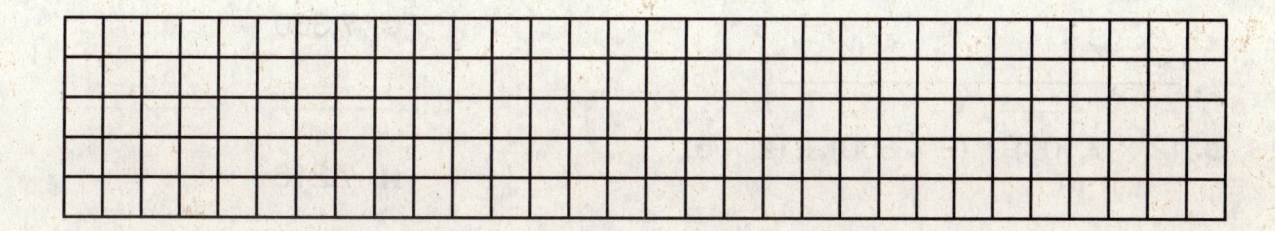

3. **Stretch Your Thinking** Find the partial products for one of your grids in Exercise 1. Then use the Distributive Property to find the product 3 × 28.

_____

_____

Enrich   E13   Grade 4

Name _____

Lesson 2.6
Enrich

Expanded Form Match-Up

Write the multiplication expression for each expanded form.
Then match the multiplication expression with its product.

1. $(7 \times 900) + (7 \times 80) + (7 \times 7)$

   _____

2. $(3 \times 5,000) + (3 \times 40) + (3 \times 8)$

   _____

3. $(8 \times 900) + (8 \times 2)$

   _____

4. $(4 \times 3,000) + (4 \times 900) + (4 \times 60) + (4 \times 2)$

   _____

5. $(2 \times 7,000) + (2 \times 800) + (2 \times 6)$

   _____

6. $(9 \times 700) + (9 \times 80) + (9 \times 5)$

   _____

A. 15,144

B. 7,065

C. 15,720

D. 6,909

E. 16,224

F. 15,848

G. 7,360

H. 7,216

I. 15,612

J. 14,172

Enrich

E14

Grade 4

© Houghton Mifflin Harcourt Publishing Company

Name _____

Lesson 2.7
Enrich

Shaping Factors

Choose one number from a circle and another number from a triangle. Then use these two numbers to write a number sentence that is true. You can use numbers more than once.

1. Find the least product.
   _____

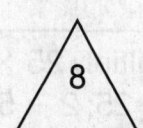

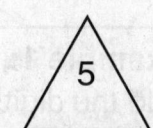

2. Find the greatest product.
   _____

3. Find the product closest to 1,050.
   _____

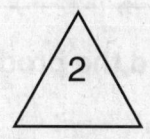

4. Find a product with an 8 in the ones place.
   _____

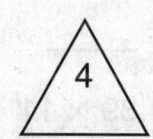

5. Find the greatest product ending in 25.
   _____

6. Find a product between 1,500 and 1,700.
   _____

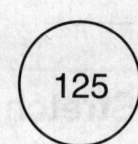

7. Find a product that contains only the digits 2 and 9.
   _____

8. Find the product with three zeros.
   _____

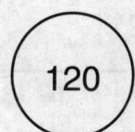

9. Find the product closest to 500.
   _____

10. Find the product closest to 2,000.
    _____

△ 8   △ 5

○ $421   △ 2

○ $583   △ 4

○ 149   ○ 125

△ 9   ○ 120

○ $374   △ 7

Enrich

E15

Grade 4

© Houghton Mifflin Harcourt Publishing Company

Name _____

Lesson 2.8
Enrich

Multiply by 11 Mentally

To find the product of a two-digit number and 11, add the digits in the two-digit number and write the sum between the two digits. If the sum is greater than 9, write the *last* digit of the sum between the two digits. Then add 1 to the *first* digit.

Example 1: Multiply 25 × 11. Add the digits in 25: 2 + 5 = 7 Place the sum, 7, between 2 and 5. So, 25 × 11 = 275.	**Example 2:** Multiply 59 × 11. Add the digits in 59: 5 + 9 = 14 Place the last digit, 4, between 5 and 9. Add 1 to the first digit: 5 + 1 = 6 So, 59 × 11 = 649.

Find the product.

1. 17 × 11

2. 32 × 11

3. 45 × 11

_____

_____

_____

4. 39 × 11

5. 67 × 11

6. 89 × 11

_____

_____

_____

7. **Stretch Your Thinking** Find a way to multiply 354 × 11 mentally. Describe your method and show that it works.

_____
_____
_____
_____
_____
_____

Name _____

Lesson 2.9
Enrich

2-Digit Roses

Draw a diagram to solve the problem.

A rose garden has 8 rows of 26 rose bushes each. In each of the first 5 rows, 7 bushes have pink roses. In each of the first 3 rows, 12 bushes have yellow roses. The rest of the bushes have red roses. How many bushes have red roses?

Read the Problem	**Solve the Problem**
What do I need to find?	**Draw a diagram and do your work here.**
I need to find the number of bushes with _____ roses.	
What information do I need to use?	
In the entire garden, there are _____ rows with _____ bushes in each row.	
There are _____ rows with _____ pink bushes in each row.	I found the total number of rose bushes. _____
	I found the number of pink rose bushes. _____
There are _____ rows with _____ yellow bushes in each row.	I found the number of yellow rose bushes. _____
How will I use the information?	
I can _____ to find the total number of bushes, the number of pink rose bushes, and the number of yellow rose bushes.	

1. What else do you need to do to solve the problem?

   _____

   _____

   _____

2. **Stretch Your Thinking** Give at least two reasons why drawing a diagram is helpful when solving a problem.

   _____

   _____

   _____

Name _____

Lesson 2.10
Enrich

Regrouping Review

Each multiplication problem below was solved using partial products. Some errors were made. Multiply using regrouping to check each answer. Describe any errors that you find.

1. Partial product	Regrouping	2. Partial product	Regrouping
72 × 8 ――― 26 + 560 ――― 586	72 × 8 ―――	65 × 9 ――― 54 + 540 ――― 594	65 × 9 ―――
Did you find any errors? If so, describe. ――――――――― ――――――――― ―――――――――		Did you find any errors? If so, describe. ――――――――― ――――――――― ―――――――――	
3. Partial product	Regrouping	4. Partial product	Regrouping
36 × 5 ――― 11 + 150 ――― 161	36 × 5 ―――	47 × 4 ――― 28 + 16 ――― 44	47 × 4 ―――
Did you find any errors? If so, describe. ――――――――― ――――――――― ―――――――――		Did you find any errors? If so, describe. ――――――――― ――――――――― ―――――――――	

5. **Stretch Your Thinking** Compare the factors and the product in Exercise 4. What information does this give you?

―――――――――――――――――――――――――――

6. **Write Math** ▶ **Explain** how you can use partial products to check products you found with regrouping.

―――――――――――――――――――――――――――

―――――――――――――――――――――――――――

Name _____   Lesson 2.11
                                Enrich

Multiplication Mystery

There's something mysterious in the water off the coast of Florida.
To discover what it is, find the products and use the decoder below.
The first letter has been done for you.

1	2	3	4	5	6	7	8	9	10	11	12	13	14	15	16	17	18	19	20	21	22	23	24	25	26
A	B	C	D	E	F	G	H	I	J	K	L	M	N	O	P	Q	R	S	T	U	V	W	X	Y	Z

1. Letter 1: 2 × 6,532

Answer: 13,064

Code: Use the ten thousands digit and the thousands digit.
13 Letter: M

2. Letter 2: 5 × 245

Answer: _____

Code: Use the thousands digit.
___ Letter: ___

3. Letter 3: 3 × 4,893

Answer: _____

Code: Use the ten thousands digit and the thousands digit.
___ Letter: ___

4. Letter 4: 7 × 198

Answer: _____

Code: Use the thousands digit.
___ Letter: ___

5. Letter 5: 6 × 3,411

Answer: _____

Code: Use the ten thousands digit and the thousands digit.
___ Letter: ___

6. Letter 6: 4 × 129

Answer: _____

Code: Use the hundreds digit.
___ Letter: ___

7. Letter 7: 8 × 730

Answer: _____

Code: Use the thousands digit.
___ Letter: ___

IT'S A M __ __ __ __ __ __ !

8. The product of 5 and another number has the code for E in its ones place. What digit could be in the ones place of the other number? **Explain.**

_____

_____

9. **Write Math** Is the product of a 4-digit number and a 1-digit number always a 5-digit number? **Explain.**

_____

_____

Enrich   E19   Grade 4
© Houghton Mifflin Harcourt Publishing Company

Name _____

Lesson 2.12
Enrich

Same Answer Multistep

Find the value of n for each exercise. Then identify the exercises that have the same answer.

1. $6 \times 36 + 3 \times 37 + 57 = n$

   _____ = n

2. $8 \times 47 + 2 \times 29 - 80 = n$

   _____ = n

3. $7 \times 45 + 4 \times 19 - 17 = n$

   _____ = n

4. $7 \times 56 + 2 \times 12 - 52 = n$

   _____ = n

5. $5 \times 52 + 6 \times 12 + 42 = n$

   _____ = n

6. $9 \times 32 + 4 \times 28 - 16 = n$

   _____ = n

7. $4 \times 46 + 3 \times 61 + 17 = n$

   _____ = n

8. $9 \times 39 + 2 \times 19 - 15 = n$

   _____ = n

9. $2 \times 98 + 8 \times 16 + 30 = n$

   _____ = n

10. $3 \times 75 + 4 \times 23 + 47 = n$

    _____ = n

11. Which exercise(s) have the same answer as Exercise 1? _____

12. Which exercise(s) have the same answer as Exercise 2? _____

13. Which exercise(s) have the same answer as Exercise 3? _____

14. **Stretch Your Thinking** What statement can you make about the equations in Exercise 4 and Exercise 10? **Explain**.

_____

_____

Enrich

E20

Grade 4

© Houghton Mifflin Harcourt Publishing Company

Name _____

Lesson 3.1
Enrich

Multiplying with Tens

Solve each problem.

1. Juice boxes come in cases of 24. A school ordered 480 juice boxes. How many cases of juice boxes did the school order?

   _____

2. John has 630 baseball cards. He sorts the cards into stacks of 30 cards. How many stacks can he make?

   _____

3. A bank received a supply of 2,000 quarters. Each roll of quarters has 40 quarters in it. How many rolls of quarters did the bank receive?

   _____

4. There are 10 tickets in each strip of carnival tickets. A total of 3,850 tickets were sold in one day. How many strips of tickets were sold that day?

   _____

5. **Write Math** ▶ **Explain** what strategy you used to solve Problem 3.

   _____
   _____
   _____
   _____

Enrich
© Houghton Mifflin Harcourt Publishing Company

E21

Grade 4

Name _____

Lesson 3.2
Enrich

Decode the Message

Use estimation to decide which product is greatest. Then write the letter of the correct answer above its place in the letter puzzle below. For example, the letter of the greatest product from Exercise 1 goes above Blank 1. The first one has been done for you.

1.	A	42 × 50	E	33 × 64	T	(48 × 56)
2.	A	12 × 15	B	11 × 14	C	10 × 13
3.	J	91 × 24	O	89 × 33	P	82 × 31
4.	K	78 × 46	R	74 × 48	E	79 × 55
5.	A	45 × 32	I	48 × 39	R	43 × 34
6.	I	25 × 26	E	23 × 27	Y	22 × 27
7.	T	50 × 48	W	56 × 42	B	51 × 44
8.	T	34 × 62	R	32 × 69	S	37 × 65
9.	N	88 × 72	P	67 × 70	M	91 × 64
10.	D	43 × 53	H	42 × 56	M	42 × 61

What is a great way to evaluate the reasonableness of an answer?

___ ___ ___ ___ ___ ___ T ___ ___ ___
4.   8.   7.   5.   10. 2.   1.   6.   3.   9.

11. **Write Math** For Exercise 10, how did you use estimation to decide which was the greatest product?

_____
_____
_____
_____

12. **Stretch Your Thinking** How could you estimate the product 253 × 93? **Explain.**

_____
_____
_____
_____

Enrich

E22

Grade 4

© Houghton Mifflin Harcourt Publishing Company

Name _____

Lesson 3.3
Enrich

The Lattice Method

Among the earliest methods of multiplication is the lattice method.

Multiply. 13 × 52

- Write one factor along the top of the lattice and the other factor along the right side.

- Multiply each digit of the factors. Record the products inside the lattice so the ones and tens are separated by a diagonal.

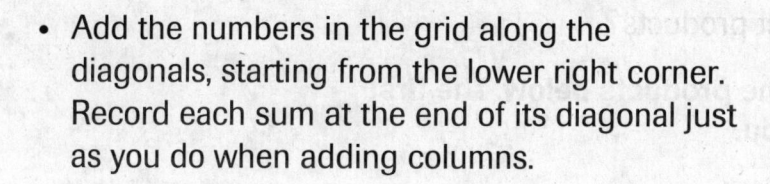

- Add the numbers in the grid along the diagonals, starting from the lower right corner. Record each sum at the end of its diagonal just as you do when adding columns.

- Read the digits down the left and across the bottom. This is the product.

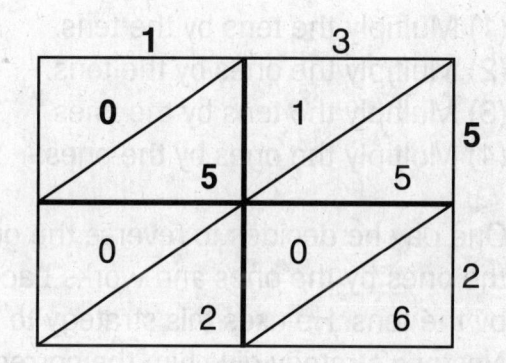

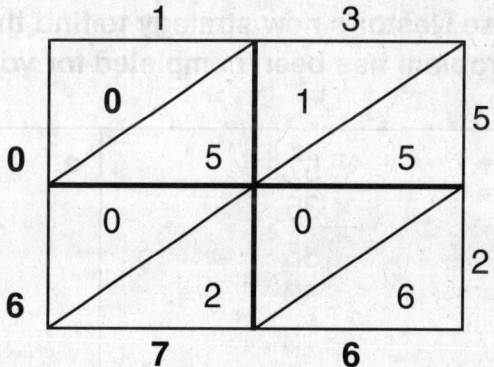

So, 13 × 52 = 676.

Use the lattice method to find the product.

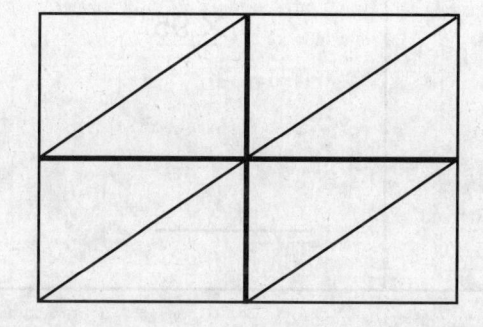

1. 31 × 22 = _____

2. 32 × 56 = _____

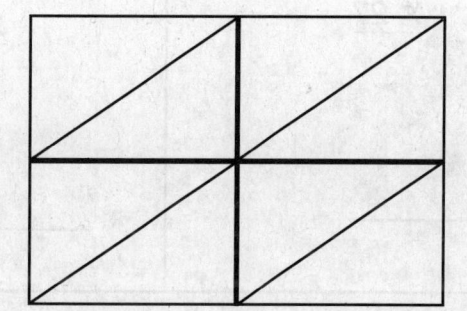

3. **Write Math** How does the lattice method use partial products to multiply?

_____

_____

_____

Enrich   E23   Grade 4
© Houghton Mifflin Harcourt Publishing Company

Name _____

Lesson 3.4
Enrich

Reverse and Record

When Nestor records 2-digit by 2-digit multiplication, he always records the partial products in the following order:

(1) Multiply the tens by the tens.
(2) Multiply the ones by the tens.
(3) Multiply the tens by the ones.
(4) Multiply the ones by the ones.

One day he decides to reverse the order. He starts by multiplying the ones by the ones and works backward to multiplying the tens by the tens. He uses this strategy to multiply some numbers. Will Nestor's strategy give him the correct products?

Use Nestor's new strategy to find the products below. The first problem has been completed for you.

1. 57 × 35 ――― 35 250 210 + 1,500 ――― 1,995	2. 31 × 22 ――― _____	3. 44 × 63 ――― _____
4. 75 × 27 ――― _____	5. 83 × 19 ――― _____	6. 59 × 95 ――― _____

7. Stretch Your Thinking How can Nestor check that his products are correct?

_____

_____

_____

Name _____

Lesson 3.5
Enrich

Multiplication Mystery

Write the multiplication problem represented by the partial products. Then write the product.

1. 800 + 280 + 60 + 21

   _____

2. 600 + 40 + 180 + 12

   _____

3. 2,000 + 280 + 300 + 42

   _____

4. 3,600 + 300 + 300 + 25

   _____

5. 2,100 + 560 + 0 + 0

   _____

6. 7,200 + 270 + 320 + 12

   _____

7. **Write Math** Which exercise did you find the most difficult to solve? **Explain**.

_____

_____

Enrich   E25   Grade 4
© Houghton Mifflin Harcourt Publishing Company

Name _____

Lesson 3.6
Enrich

Product Pairs

Tatum and Elija are doing their homework together. They need to find two problems that have the same product. Help Tatum and Elija finish their homework by finding the product in the first problem. Then find the unknown digit in the second problem that will make the products equal.

1. 34 × 15 = 510   30 × 1[7] = 510

2. 46 × 25 = 1,150   50 × 2[3] = 1,150

3. 54 × 39 = 2,106   81 × 2[6] = 2,106

4. 75 × 27 = 2,025   45 × 4[5] = 2,025

5. 44 × 32 = 1,408   88 × 1[6] = 1,408

6. 90 × 24 = 2,160   80 × 2[7] = 2,160

7. 64 × 49 = 3,136   56 × 5[6] = 3,136

8. 38 × 35 = 1,330   95 × 1[4] = 1,330

9. **Stretch Your Thinking** Show two problems that each have two 2-digit factors and the same product.

_____

_____

Enrich   E26   Grade 4
© Houghton Mifflin Harcourt Publishing Company

Name _____

Lesson 3.7
Enrich

Pastry Chef's Problem

A pastry chef is making lemon squares and pumpkin squares for a special event. Here are the facts the chef knows.

- Each square is to measure 1 inch by 1 inch.
- There are to be an equal number of each type of square.
- All squares need to be baked at the same time.
- The chef has only the pans shown below.

1. The chef wants to make the greatest number of squares possible while using only 4 pans. Which pans should the chef choose?

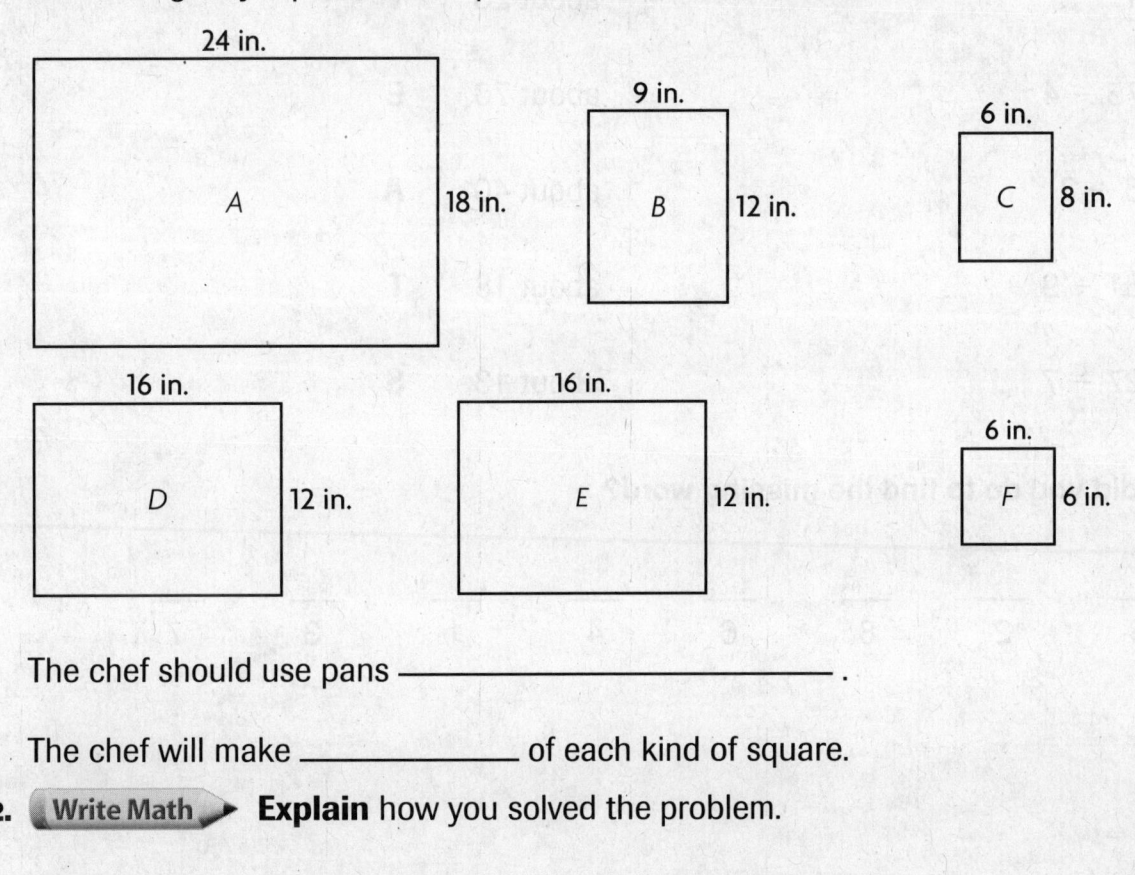

A: 24 in. by 18 in.
B: 9 in. by 12 in.
C: 6 in. by 8 in.
D: 16 in. by 12 in.
E: 16 in. by 12 in.
F: 6 in. by 6 in.

The chef should use pans _____.

The chef will make _____ of each kind of square.

2. **Write Math** **Explain** how you solved the problem.

_____
_____
_____
_____
_____
_____

E27

Name _____

Lesson 4.1
Enrich

Estimating Quotients

Match each quotient with its best estimate. Then write the letter of the estimate on the appropriate blank to answer the question below.

1. 342 ÷ 8	about 50	E
2. 93 ÷ 7	about 15	M
3. 125 ÷ 6	about 12	I
4. 74 ÷ 5	about 20	T
5. 275 ÷ 4	about 70	E
6. 35 ÷ 3	about 40	A
7. 481 ÷ 9	about 18	T
8. 127 ÷ 7	about 13	S

What did you do to find the missing word?

__ __ __ __ __ __ __ __
5 2 8 6 4 1 3 7

Name _____

Lesson 4.2
Enrich

Riddle Time

Use the clues to solve the riddles below. You will need to know the name for each part of a division equation. Use the division problem at the right as a reminder.

QUOTIENT   REMAINDER
         9 r1
        4)37
DIVISOR   DIVIDEND

1. My divisor is 5.
   I am greater than 4 × 5.
   I am less than 5 × 5.
   My remainder is 1.
   What dividend am I?

   _____

2. My divisor is 9.
   I am greater than 7 × 9.
   I am less than 8 × 9.
   My remainder is 7.
   What dividend am I?

   _____

3. My divisor is 8.
   I am less than 30.
   I am greater than 3 × 8.
   My remainder is 5.
   What dividend am I?

   _____

4. My divisor is 6.
   I am less than 60.
   I am greater than 8 × 6.
   I have no remainder.
   What dividend am I?

   _____

5. My dividend is 50.
   My remainder is 1.
   I am an odd number.
   What divisor am I?

   _____

6. My dividend is 8 times as large as my divisor.
   I am an even number less than 15.
   What quotient am I?

   _____

7. My remainder is 8.
   My dividend is 80.
   I am a 1-digit number.
   What divisor am I?

   _____

8. My dividend is 24.
   I am 2 more than my quotient.
   I have no remainder.
   What divisor am I?

   _____

9. **Write Math** ▶ Use Exercises 1–8 as models to write your own division number riddle.

_____

_____

Enrich   E29   Grade 4
© Houghton Mifflin Harcourt Publishing Company

Name _____ Lesson 4.3
Enrich

Remainder Jeopardy

Read each scenario. Use the scenario to write questions that would have the given answers.

1. There are 52 students in the fourth grade. Each minivan can hold 6 students. The students are going on a field trip.

   8 _____

   9 _____

   4 _____

2. Six friends are going on a hike. Becky made 64 ounces of trail mix.

   $10\frac{4}{6}$ _____

   4 _____

3. **Write Math** Why is it important to read division problems carefully before giving the answer?

   _____
   _____
   _____

Enrich   E30   Grade 4
© Houghton Mifflin Harcourt Publishing Company

Name _____

Lesson 4.4
Enrich

Dividend Riddles

Solve each riddle.

1. When divided by 5, I am 60. When divided by 6, I am 50. What number am I?

   _____

2. When divided by 3, I am 700. When divided by 7, I am 300. What number am I?

   _____

3. When divided by 8, I am 70. When divided by 7, I am 80. What number am I?

   _____

4. When divided by 7, I am 400. When divided by 4, I am 700. What number am I?

   _____

5. When divided by 6, I am 200. When divided by 4, I am 300. What number am I?

   _____

6. When divided by 8, I am 30. When divided by 6, I am 40. What number am I?

   _____

7. **Stretch Your Thinking** Find the sum of the six answers to the riddles. Write your own riddle so that the answer is this sum.

   _____

   _____

   _____

Enrich
E31
Grade 4
© Houghton Mifflin Harcourt Publishing Company

Name _____

Lesson 4.5
Enrich

Make the Best Estimate

One of the division expressions in columns A, B, and C is the best match for the Estimate column. Circle the best choice for each.

Estimate	A	B	C
1. 70	408 ÷ 7	8)545	816 ÷ 9
2. 80	3)251	342 ÷ 5	477 ÷ 7
3. 90	332 ÷ 5	8)628	9)780
4. 40	9)350	423 ÷ 8	538 ÷ 9
5. 100	410 ÷ 2	593 ÷ 6	4)849
6. 400	4)1,584	5)1,126	712 ÷ 3
7. 200	2,384 ÷ 5	3,006 ÷ 8	1,742 ÷ 9
8. 700	2,663 ÷ 5	6)3,411	7)5,026
9. 300	2)532	4)767	2)289
10. 120	628 ÷ 8	3)296	483 ÷ 4
11. 50	115 ÷ 4	4)198	317 ÷ 5
12. 20	8)274	221 ÷ 7	6)141
13. 900	8,250 ÷ 9	5,740 ÷ 8	2,992 ÷ 4
14. 150	6)909	8)1,040	7)881
15. 60	256 ÷ 6	189 ÷ 3	182 ÷ 5

16. **Write Math** What strategy did you use to help you choose the best match?

17. **Stretch Your Thinking** Create three of your own division expressions as estimates for Exercise 15. Circle the choice that has the best estimate.

Name _____

Lesson 4.6
Enrich

True or Not True?

The Associative Property of Multiplication states that when you change the grouping of factors, the product remains the same: (3 × 4) × 5 = 12 × 5, or 60, and 3 × (4 × 5) = 3 × 20, or 60.

**Is the Associative Property also true for division?
Complete Exercises 1–4.**

1. (8 ÷ 4) ÷ 1 = _____ and 8 ÷ (4 ÷ 1) = _____

2. (10 ÷ 2) ÷ 1 = _____ and 10 ÷ (2 ÷ 1) = _____

3. When you changed the grouping in Exercises 1 and 2, what happened to the quotient?

   _____

4. Now use the numbers 2, 4, and 8 to write and evaluate a division expression. Then change the grouping of the numbers and evaluate the new expression.

   _____
   _____

5. When you changed the grouping in Exercise 3, what happened to the quotient?

   _____

6. **Write Math** Is the Associative Property true for division? **Explain**.

   _____
   _____
   _____
   _____

Name _____

Lesson 4.7
Enrich

Subtraction Situations

Each situation below involves repeated subtraction. Read each situation. Use the given information to solve the related division problem. Explain your reasoning.

1. There are 51 fourth-graders going on a field trip. One group of 16 students rides in one van. A second group of 16 students rides in a second van. A third group of 16 students rides in a third van. The 3 students who are left ride in a car.

   Find the quotient. 51 ÷ 8

2. Kate bakes 144 cookies for a bake sale. She places 3 cookies in one bag, 3 cookies in a second bag, and so on, until there are no cookies left. She has 48 bags of 3 cookies each.

   Find the quotient. 144 ÷ 9

_____
_____
_____
_____
_____

3. **Write Math** ▶ Describe how the given situations helped you solve the division problems.

_____
_____
_____
_____

Name _____

Lesson 4.8
Enrich

Special Delivery

Mailbox #2 only accepts letters with numbers that can be evenly divided by 2.
Mailbox #3 only accepts letters with numbers that can be evenly divided by 3.
Mailbox #5 only accepts letters with numbers that can be evenly divided by 5.

1. Deliver each letter by writing each number below the correct mailbox. Some letters will be undeliverable.

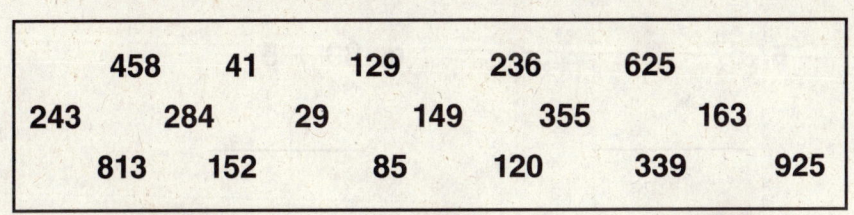

   458   41   129   236   625
   243   284   29   149   355   163
   813   152   85   120   339   925

   #2   #3   #5

   _____ _____ _____
   _____ _____ _____
   _____ _____ _____
   _____ _____ _____
   _____ _____ _____

2. **Write Math** Could any letter be delivered to all three mailboxes? **Explain** your reasoning.

   _____
   _____
   _____

Name _____

Lesson 4.9
Enrich

Division Drying

To find the answer to the riddle, complete each division.
Then use the KEY to find the answer to the riddle.

1. 78 ÷ 6

   ____

2. 58 ÷ 3

   ____

3. 92 ÷ 4

   ____

4. 88 ÷ 7

   ____

5. 57 ÷ 2

   ____

6. 89 ÷ 5

   ____

KEY:

A	D	E	L	O	T	U	V	W
13	23 r1	28 r1	17 r4	23	19 r1	17 r2	16 r2	12 r4

Riddle: The more I dry, the wetter I get. What am I?

__ __ __ __ __ __
1   2   3   4   5   6

7. **Stretch Your Thinking** Make up a new division problem for Exercise 2 so that when using the quotient and the key, the result will be the answer to this riddle: "What is the difference between SHELL and SHALL?"

_____

_____

Enrich
E36
Grade 4

© Houghton Mifflin Harcourt Publishing Company

Lesson 4.10
Enrich

How Many Digits?

Circle how many digits will be in the quotient. Find the quotient to check that you are correct. Then, look at the riddle below. To answer the riddle, write the letter of the number you circled on the line above the exercise number.

1. 346 ÷ 2 = _____
   1 = P   2 = R   3 = N

2. 108 ÷ 9 = _____
   1 = T   2 = A   3 = C

3. 652 ÷ 4 = _____
   1 = L   2 = I   3 = H

4. 210 ÷ 5 = _____
   1 = R   2 = S   3 = N

5. 120 ÷ 8 = _____
   1 = S   2 = C   3 = W

6. 162 ÷ 6 = _____
   1 = G   2 = E   3 = J

7. 420 ÷ 7 = _____
   1 = C   2 = M   3 = E

8. 444 ÷ 4 = _____
   1 = K   2 = E   3 = I

What can run but cannot walk?

___ ___ ___ ___ ___ ___ ___ ___
 7   2   5   3   8   1   6   4

Enrich   E37   Grade 4
© Houghton Mifflin Harcourt Publishing Company

Name _____

Lesson 4.11
Enrich

What Is Left Over?

Find the "leftover" in each situation. Then use the code key to see which letter matches each of your answers. Write the letters in order of the exercises to find the answer to the riddle.

1. Jude puts 6 lemons in each bag. If he has 170 lemons, how many will be left over?

   _____

2. Selena has a piece of ribbon that is 130 inches long. If she wants to make bracelets that are 9 inches long, how many inches of ribbon will be left over?

   _____

3. Justin prepares 229 hamburgers for a company picnic. If buns come in packages of 8, how many will be left over?

   _____

4. Mrs. Bradley has $204 to divide equally between her 7 grandchildren. How many dollars will she have left over?

   _____

5. Mr. White has 115 tulips for bouquets. He puts 9 tulips in each bouquet. How many tulips will be left over?

   _____

1	2	3	4	5	6	7	8
G	F	E	L	A	N	S	T

What flies around all day but never goes anywhere?

_____

It's a Riddle!

Solve each problem. Look for the answer in the riddle below and write the letter of the problem on the line. Not all letters will be used.

C	Maria takes 24 photos at the circus and 72 photos on her vacation. If each page in her scrapbook can hold 6 photos, how many pages can Maria fill?	**I**	Carmen and Wayne sell 25 birdhouses at a craft fair. They share the money equally. If each birdhouse costs $14, how much money will Carmen and Wayne each receive?
R	José uses 3 flowers for each corsage he makes. He has orders for 18 corsages each from two different stores. How many flowers will he need?	**L**	Mr. Davis sells sleeping bags. He has 30 red sleeping bags and 26 green sleeping bags to put on shelves. Each shelf can hold 8 sleeping bags. How many shelves can he fill?
Y	Taren makes 62 chocolate chip cookies and 74 oatmeal cookies. If she places 8 cookies on a plate for the bake sale, how many plates will Taren need?	**T**	Keisha bought 10 bags of apples. There are 15 apples in each bag. If Keisha repacks the apples into 5 bags, how many apples will be in each bag?
N	Chan and his two sisters make and sell jewelry. They sell each piece of jewelry for $9 and agree to share the money equally. If they sell 38 pieces of jewelry in all, how much money will each person receive?	**E**	Linh orders 16 blueberry muffins and 24 cranberry muffins from a bakery. The bakery places 8 muffins in each package. How many packages will Linh have to pick up?

Which city has no people?

 E   L   E   C   T   R   I   C   I   T   Y
___ ___ ___ ___ ___ ___ ___ ___ ___ ___ ___
 5   7   5   16 30 108 175 16 175 30 17

Name _____

Lesson 5.1
Enrich

Festive Factors

Ms. Ramirez is a professional party planner. One of her tasks is to arrange the seating at tables. Ms. Ramirez likes to have the same number of party guests seated at each table.

For each number of guests below, use factors to determine all the ways Ms. Ramirez can arrange tables and chairs to have the same number of guests at each table. You do not have to include the factor 1 and the number itself.

1. 24 guests

_____

_____

_____

2. 56 guests

_____

_____

_____

3. **Write Math** Two factors that make a product are sometimes called a factor pair. Describe how using factor pairs helped you solve the problems.

_____

_____

_____

Name _____

Lesson 5.2
Enrich

Invisible Divisible

Use the clues to find all possibilities for the unknown digit in each number.

1. The number below has 2 as a factor. What could the unknown digit be?

   5,83 ■

   _____

2. The number below has 4 as a factor. What could the unknown digit be?

   3,2 ■ 6

   _____

3. The number below has 5 as a factor. What could the unknown digit be?

   1,9 ■ 5

   _____

4. The number below has 9 as a factor. What could the unknown digit be?

   6,30 ■

   _____

5. The number below has 6 as a factor. What could the unknown digit be?

   7,71 ■

   _____

6. The number below has 3 as a factor. What could the unknown digit be?

   4, ■ 11

   _____

7. The number below has 3 and 5 as factors. What could the unknown digit be?

   6,1 ■ 5

   _____

8. The number below has 2 and 9 as factors. What could the unknown digit be?

   2,3 ■ 6

   _____

9. **Stretch Your Thinking** A number is divisible by 2 if the last digit is divisible by 2. A number is divisible by 4 if the last two digits form a number divisible by 4. A number is divisible by 8 if the last three digits form a number divisible by 8. Describe a possible pattern in the divisibility rules. Then test each of the following numbers for divisibility by 8.

   3,488   5,614   4,320   3,052

   _____

   _____

   _____

Enrich

E41

Grade 4

© Houghton Mifflin Harcourt Publishing Company

Name _____

Lesson 5.3
Enrich

Common Ground

Find common factors to solve.

1. Desiree has 100 pink, 80 blue, and 120 purple beads. She puts all of the beads into jars equally. Each jar has one type of bead. How many beads can she put in one jar?

   _____

2. Sam has 50 blue and 150 red marbles. She puts all of the marbles into bags equally. Each bag has one type of marble. How many marbles can she put in one bag?

   _____

3. The table shows the number of students in each grade at Bayside School. Mrs. Anderson wants to put students in equal rows during an assembly. Each row has students from the same grade. How many students can she put in one row?

Fifth	Sixth	Seventh	Eighth
50	25	75	100

   _____

4. The table shows the number of instruments a music company has in stock. The company discounts the same number of each type of instrument each month. How many instruments can be discounted in a month?

Trumpet	Clarinet	Flute	Drum
88	42	100	26

   _____

5. **Stretch Your Thinking** Jill wrote three numbers on the board. A common factor of the three numbers is 18. List three possible numbers. Tell how you chose the numbers.

   _____

   _____

   _____

Enrich
E42
Grade 4
© Houghton Mifflin Harcourt Publishing Company

Name _____

Lesson 5.4
Enrich

Multiple Dates

On January 1, 2011, the Petersons began a new allowance program for their four children:

> Every third day, beginning January 3, Adrian will get his allowance.
> Every fourth day, beginning January 4, Beth will get her allowance.
> Every fifth day, beginning January 5, Zoe will get her allowance.
> Every seventh day, beginning January 7, Eddie will get his allowance.

1. What is the first day that Adrian and Beth will get their allowances on the same day?

   _____

2. What is the first day that Beth and Zoe will get their allowances on the same day?

   _____

3. What is the first day that Adrian and Eddie will get their allowances on the same day?

   _____

4. What is the first day that Adrian, Beth, and Zoe will get their allowances on the same day?

   _____

5. **Stretch Your Thinking** How many days will it be until all four children will get their allowances on the same day? **Explain.**

   _____

   _____

   _____

Name _____

Lesson 5.5
Enrich

Prime Search

All the prime numbers from 1 to 100 are listed below.

2, 3, 5, 7, 11, 13, 17, 19, 23, 29, 31, 37, 41, 43, 47, 53, 59, 61, 67, 71, 73, 79, 83, 89, 97

1. Find the prime numbers from 101 to 200.

- First draw a line through all the multiples of 2.
- Then draw a line through all the multiples of 3, then all the multiples of 5, and continue until you have drawn lines through all the multiples of prime numbers less than 100.
- The remaining numbers are the prime numbers from 101 to 200. List these below the table.

101	102	103	104	105	106	107	108	109	110
111	112	113	114	115	116	117	118	119	120
121	122	123	124	125	126	127	128	129	130
131	132	133	134	135	136	137	138	139	140
141	142	143	144	145	146	147	148	149	150
151	152	153	154	155	156	157	158	159	160
161	162	163	164	165	166	167	168	169	170
171	172	173	174	175	176	177	178	179	180
181	182	183	184	185	186	187	188	189	190
191	192	193	194	195	196	197	198	199	200

_____

_____

2. The number 143 has two lines through it, first as a multiple of 11 and second as a multiple of 13; so, 143 is the product of two prime numbers. Find another number that is the product of two different prime numbers greater than 7.

3. **Write Math** **Explain** how you can find all the prime numbers from 201 to 1,000.

Enrich E44 Grade 4
© Houghton Mifflin Harcourt Publishing Company

Name _____

Lesson 5.6
Enrich

Pattern Perfect

Write a rule for each pattern. Then use your rule to find the next two terms in the pattern.

1. 1, 4, 9, 16, 25, 36, 49, . . .

   _____

   _____

2. 1, 1, 2, 3, 5, 8, 13, 21, 34, . . .

   _____

   _____

3. 1, 3, 6, 10, 15, 21, 28, 36, . . .

   _____

   _____

4. **Stretch Your Thinking** Find a rule for the pattern below without using inverse operations (such as "subtract 4, add 4").

   8, 4, 8, 4, 8, 4, 8, 4, . . .

   Then create a similar pattern of your own and give its rule.

   _____

   _____

   _____

Enrich   E45   Grade 4

© Houghton Mifflin Harcourt Publishing Company

Name _____

Lesson 6.1
Enrich

Equivalent Fraction Find

In the grid below, circle seven fractions that are equivalent to $\frac{2}{4}$.

$\frac{2}{6}$	$\frac{7}{12}$	$\frac{1}{4}$	$\frac{8}{10}$	$\frac{7}{8}$	$\frac{4}{5}$
$\frac{6}{12}$	$\frac{3}{10}$	$\frac{2}{3}$	$\frac{5}{12}$	$\frac{2}{8}$	$\frac{1}{2}$
$\frac{2}{5}$	$\frac{40}{100}$	$\frac{5}{6}$	$\frac{3}{12}$	$\frac{50}{100}$	$\frac{10}{12}$
$\frac{4}{8}$	$\frac{8}{12}$	$\frac{5}{10}$	$\frac{60}{100}$	$\frac{3}{8}$	$\frac{5}{8}$
$\frac{3}{4}$	$\frac{6}{10}$	$\frac{2}{12}$	$\frac{4}{6}$	$\frac{8}{16}$	$\frac{3}{5}$
$\frac{1}{5}$	$\frac{3}{6}$	$\frac{6}{8}$	$\frac{4}{12}$	$\frac{7}{10}$	$\frac{1}{8}$

1. Find two fractions in the grid that are not equivalent to $\frac{2}{4}$, but that are equivalent to each other.

   _____

2. **Write Math** ▶ Describe how you determined which fractions in the grid are equivalent to $\frac{2}{4}$.

   _____

   _____

   _____

Name _____

Lesson 6.2
Enrich

Equivalent Art

Write the fraction represented by the shaded part of each design.
Then write 3 fractions that are equivalent to that fraction.

1.  ★★★★★★

Fraction represented by the shaded part of the design:
_____

Three equivalent fractions:
_____

2.  ◆◆◇

Fraction represented by the shaded part of the design:
_____

Three equivalent fractions:
_____

3.  ♥♥♥♡♡

Fraction represented by the shaded part of the design:
_____

Three equivalent fractions:
_____

4. 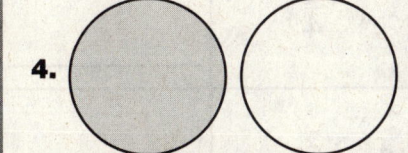 ●○

Fraction represented by the shaded part of the design:
_____

Three equivalent fractions:
_____

5. 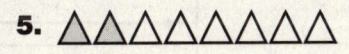 △△△△△△△△

Fraction represented by the shaded part of the design:
_____

Three equivalent fractions:
_____

6. 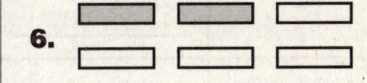 ▬▬▭ ▭▭▭

Fraction represented by the shaded part of the design:
_____

Three equivalent fractions:
_____

7. Stretch Your Thinking There is a relationship between the shaded part of each design and the unshaded part. Describe this relationship.

_____

_____

_____

Enrich   E47   Grade 4
© Houghton Mifflin Harcourt Publishing Company

Name _____

Lesson 6.3
Enrich

To Simplify or Not To Simplify?

Tell whether each fraction below is in simplest form. If a fraction is in simplest form, write *Simplest form*. If a fraction is not in simplest form, write it in simplest form.

1. $\frac{4}{8}$ _____	2. $\frac{10}{12}$ _____	3. $\frac{4}{5}$ _____
4. $\frac{9}{10}$ _____	5. $\frac{2}{3}$ _____	6. $\frac{19}{100}$ _____
7. $\frac{6}{8}$ _____	8. $\frac{1}{6}$ _____	9. $\frac{7}{12}$ _____
10. $\frac{5}{12}$ _____	11. $\frac{4}{6}$ _____	12. $\frac{3}{4}$ _____
13. $\frac{2}{5}$ _____	14. $\frac{2}{8}$ _____	15. $\frac{5}{8}$ _____
16. $\frac{3}{10}$ _____	17. $\frac{47}{100}$ _____	18. $\frac{4}{12}$ _____

19. **Write Math** Describe how you determined which fractions were already in simplest form.

_____

_____

_____

Name _____   Lesson 6.4
Enrich

Common Denominator Combos

For each group of fractions below, find a common denominator. Then write the group of fractions as a group of fractions with a common denominator.

Fractions	Common Denominator	Equivalent Fractions
1. $\frac{2}{3}, \frac{3}{4}, \frac{5}{6}$	_____	_____
2. $\frac{5}{8}, \frac{1}{3}, \frac{1}{2}$	_____	_____
3. $\frac{2}{3}, \frac{7}{9}, \frac{1}{6}$	_____	_____
4. $\frac{4}{9}, \frac{5}{6}, \frac{1}{4}$	_____	_____
5. $\frac{1}{5}, \frac{2}{3}, \frac{1}{2}, \frac{5}{6}$	_____	_____

6. **Write Math** Compare the processes for finding common denominators for two, three, and four fractions.

_____
_____
_____
_____

Enrich   E49   Grade 4
© Houghton Mifflin Harcourt Publishing Company

Name _____

**Lesson 6.5
Enrich**

Factors, Fractions, and Fruit

Callie is starting a fruit basket business. The largest fruit basket will contain 30 pieces of fruit. Other baskets may contain fewer, but at least 12, pieces of fruit. In every basket, $\frac{1}{2}$ of the pieces of fruit must be apples, $\frac{1}{3}$ must be oranges, and $\frac{1}{6}$ must be bananas. What combinations of pieces of fruit represent all the possible fruit baskets Callie can make?

Fill in the table to solve the problem.

Total Pieces of Fruit in Basket	Common Denominator	Fractions	Combination of Fruit
1.			
2.			
3.			
4.			

5. **Write Math** There is a pattern in the combinations as the total number of pieces of fruit increases. Describe any patterns you notice.

_____
_____
_____
_____

Name _____

Lesson 6.6
Enrich

At the Pet Store

Use the table for 1–8.

Types of Pets in the Pet Store					
Pets	Puppies	Fish	Turtles	Parakeets	Rabbits
Fraction of Total Number of Pets	$\frac{1}{4}$	$\frac{1}{3}$	$\frac{1}{12}$	$\frac{1}{6}$	$\frac{2}{12}$

1. The pet store has the same number of which two animals?

   _____

2. Are there more puppies or more fish?

   _____

3. Are there more parakeets or more turtles?

   _____

4. Are there more puppies or more rabbits?

   _____

5. Are there more turtles or more rabbits?

   _____

6. The pet store has the most of which animal?

   _____

7. The pet store has the fewest of which animal?

   _____

8. Are there more fish or more turtles?

   _____

9. **Stretch Your Thinking** Suppose a pet store owner has 12 pets and wants $\frac{1}{2}$ of the total number of pets to be fish. How many fish does the owner need? Explain how you know.

   _____

   _____

   _____

Enrich E51 Grade 4
© Houghton Mifflin Harcourt Publishing Company

Name _____

Lesson 6.7
Enrich

Parts of a Project

For a project, Damian, Tim, and Keisha split the work. Damian completed $\frac{1}{6}$ of the project, Keisha completed $\frac{7}{12}$ of the project, and Tim completed $\frac{1}{4}$ of the project. Who completed the greatest part, the second greatest part, and the least part of the project?

1. **Fill in the table to solve the problem.**

Name	Fraction of the Project	Common Denominator	Fraction with Common Denominator
Damian	$\frac{1}{6}$		
Keisha	$\frac{7}{12}$		
Tim	$\frac{1}{4}$		

2. Write the fractions in order from greatest to least.

_____

3. Write the names of the students in the order starting with who completed the greatest part of the project to who completed the least part of the project.

_____

4. **Write Math** There is a relationship between all of the numerators in the fractions with the common denominator. Describe the relationship.

_____

_____

_____

_____

Enrich

E52

Grade 4

© Houghton Mifflin Harcourt Publishing Company

Name _____

Lesson 6.8
Enrich

Filling Cups

Leo, Steve, and Isabelle each have identical cups to fill with water. Leo fills his cup $\frac{3}{4}$ full, and Steve fills his cup $\frac{2}{5}$ full. Isabel is asked to fill her cup so that the amount of water in her cup is between the amounts of water in Leo's and Steve's cups. What could be the amount of water Isabelle puts in her cup?

Fill in the table to solve the problem.

Name	Fraction of Cup Filled	Common Denominator	Fraction with Common Denominator
Leo	$\frac{3}{4}$		
Steve	$\frac{2}{5}$		

1. Write the fractions in order from least to greatest.

    _____

2. Use your common denominator. What fractions with this denominator are between $\frac{3}{4}$ and $\frac{2}{5}$?

    _____

3. Can Isabelle use these fractions to decide how much water to put in her cup?

    _____

    _____

4. **Stretch Your Thinking** How can you find a fraction between the fractions $\frac{14}{20}$ and $\frac{15}{20}$?

    _____

    _____

Name _____

Lesson 7.1
Enrich

Fraction Fun

Solve each problem.

1. Gina ate $\frac{1}{6}$ of an apple pie. Greg ate $\frac{1}{2}$ of the same pie. How much of the apple pie was left?

   _____

2. So far, John has run $\frac{1}{4}$ of the way to school and walked $\frac{3}{8}$ of the way. What fraction of the distance to school does John have left?

   _____

3. Ann, Nan, and Jan snacked on a plate of fruit slices while doing their homework. Ann ate $\frac{1}{5}$ of the fruit slices, Nan ate $\frac{2}{5}$ of the fruit slices, and Jan ate $\frac{1}{5}$ of the fruit slices. What fraction of the fruit slices are left on the plate?

   _____

4. While watching a movie, Ned, Fred, and Jed shared a bowl of popcorn. Ned ate $\frac{1}{2}$ of the popcorn, Fred ate $\frac{1}{4}$ of the popcorn, and Jed ate $\frac{1}{8}$ of the popcorn. What fraction of the bowl of popcorn is left?

   _____

5. In a grid of squares, Alice colored $\frac{3}{4}$ of the squares blue. She colored $\frac{1}{8}$ of the squares red. She colored the rest of the squares yellow. What fraction of the squares did Alice color yellow?

   _____

6. Pierre bounced a ball for $\frac{1}{3}$ of his recess time. He threw the ball in the air and caught it $\frac{3}{6}$ of the time. He carried the ball the rest of the time. For what fraction of his recess time did he carry the ball?

   _____

7. **Write Math** How did you solve Problem 6? **Explain.**

   _____

   _____

   _____

   _____

Enrich
© Houghton Mifflin Harcourt Publishing Company

Grade 4

Lesson 7.2
Enrich

Name _____

Mixed-Up Sums

Match each fraction on the left with an addition problem on the right.

1. $\frac{7}{8}$ $\frac{3}{8} + \frac{2}{8} + \frac{1}{8}$

2. $\frac{6}{10}$ $\frac{2}{10} + \frac{2}{10} + \frac{2}{10}$

3. $\frac{4}{8}$ $\frac{1}{10} + \frac{3}{10} + \frac{2}{10} + \frac{3}{10}$

4. $\frac{9}{10}$ $\frac{1}{8} + \frac{5}{8} + \frac{1}{8}$

5. $\frac{6}{8}$ $\frac{1}{10} + \frac{3}{10} + \frac{2}{10} + \frac{1}{10}$

6. $\frac{7}{10}$ $\frac{1}{8} + \frac{1}{8} + \frac{2}{8}$

7. **Stretch Your Thinking** Write another possible sum for Exercise 4.

_____

8. **Stretch Your Thinking** Write another possible sum for Exercise 5. Use $\frac{1}{4}$ for one of the addends. Explain how you found your answer.

_____

_____

Enrich   E55   Grade 4
© Houghton Mifflin Harcourt Publishing Company

Name _____

Lesson 7.3
Enrich

Sum Fractions!

Find the two fractions that have the sum shown. Use each fraction only once. Use fraction strips to help.

1. The sum is $\frac{7}{8}$.

   | $\frac{1}{8}$ | $\frac{2}{8}$ | $\frac{3}{8}$ | $\frac{5}{8}$ | $\frac{7}{8}$ |

   _____

2. The sum is $\frac{5}{6}$.

   | $\frac{1}{6}$ | $\frac{2}{6}$ | $\frac{3}{6}$ | $\frac{5}{6}$ | $\frac{8}{6}$ |

   _____

3. The sum is $\frac{9}{12}$.

   | $\frac{1}{12}$ | $\frac{2}{12}$ | $\frac{3}{12}$ | $\frac{5}{12}$ | $\frac{8}{12}$ |

   _____

4. The sum is $\frac{6}{10}$.

   | $\frac{1}{10}$ | $\frac{2}{10}$ | $\frac{3}{10}$ | $\frac{4}{10}$ | $\frac{6}{10}$ |

   _____

5. The sum is $\frac{4}{4}$.

   | $\frac{1}{4}$ | $\frac{2}{4}$ | $\frac{3}{4}$ | $\frac{5}{4}$ | $\frac{7}{4}$ |

   _____

6. The sum is 1.

   | $\frac{1}{5}$ | $\frac{2}{5}$ | $\frac{3}{5}$ | $\frac{5}{5}$ | $\frac{6}{5}$ |

   _____

7. **Stretch Your Thinking** Suppose you could use a fraction more than once. What other answer could you find for Exercise 5? Which other exercise would have more than one answer?

   _____

8. **Write Math** Write a fraction sum problem similar to the ones above.

   _____

Enrich
E56
Grade 4

© Houghton Mifflin Harcourt Publishing Company

Name _____

Lesson 7.4
Enrich

Fraction Food

The Foodly family just finished dinner. Help them determine how much food is left. Shade the models to help.

1. The lasagna was cut into 12 equal pieces. The Foodly family ate 7 pieces of lasagna. What fraction of the lasagna is left?

   _____ twelfths − _____ twelfths = _____ twelfths or _____

2. The green bean casserole was divided into 6 equal servings. The Foodly family ate 5 servings. What fraction of the casserole is left?

   _____ sixths − _____ sixths = _____ sixth or _____

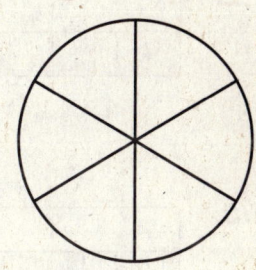

3. The gelatin salad was cut into 8 equal servings. The Foodly family ate 6 servings of the salad. What fraction of the gelatin salad is left?

   _____ eighths − _____ eighths = _____ eighths or _____

4. The pumpkin bread was cut into 10 equal pieces. The Foodly family ate 5 pieces. What fraction of the pumpkin bread is left?

   _____ tenths − _____ tenths = _____ tenths or _____

5. **Stretch Your Thinking** The Foodly family had 2 pans of cornbread. Each pan was cut into 5 equal pieces. They ate only 2 pieces. What fraction of the pans of cornbread is left? Draw a model to help.

_____

Enrich   E57   Grade 4
© Houghton Mifflin Harcourt Publishing Company

Name _____

Lesson 7.5
Enrich

Fraction Equations

Record the equation shown by the model. Write the answer in simplest form.

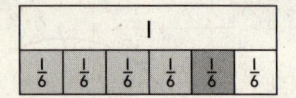

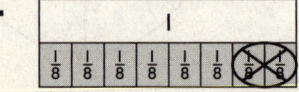

1. [model: 10/10 bar with 2/10 crossed out] — X: $\frac{8}{10} - \frac{2}{10} = \frac{6}{10} = \frac{3}{5}$

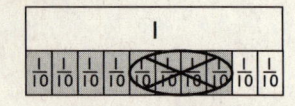

2. [model: 6 sixths, some shaded] — H

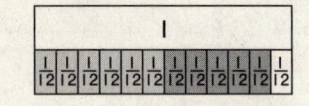

3. [model: 8/8 bar with pieces crossed out] — S

4. [model: 12 twelfths] — I

5. [model: 4 fourths shaded] — T

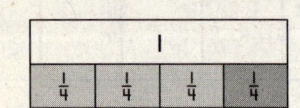

To answer the riddle, write the letter above its answer.

Why did all the fractions think $\frac{1}{6}$ was special?

Because it had a ___ ___ ___ ___ ___ sense!
$\qquad\quad\ \ \frac{3}{4}\ \ \ \frac{11}{12}\ \ \ \frac{2}{5}\ \ \ 1\ \ \ \frac{5}{6}$

Enrich   E58   Grade 4
© Houghton Mifflin Harcourt Publishing Company

Lesson 7.6
Enrich

The Rename Game

Find the missing number.

1. $51\dfrac{\square}{5} = \dfrac{256}{5}$

2. $72\dfrac{\square}{3} = \dfrac{218}{3}$

3. $\square\dfrac{1}{2} = \dfrac{422}{4}$

4. $\square\dfrac{1}{4} = \dfrac{506}{8}$

5. $102\dfrac{5}{12} = \dfrac{\square}{12}$

6. $37\dfrac{1}{3} = \dfrac{224}{\square}$

7. **Write Math** Tell how you rename fractions greater than 1 as mixed numbers and mixed numbers as fractions greater than 1.

_____

_____

_____

_____

8. **Stretch Your Thinking** Is it possible for two fractions greater than 1 that have different numerators and denominators to be renamed as the same mixed number? Give an example.

_____

_____

Name _____

Lesson 7.7
Enrich

Finding Mixed Numbers

Solve each problem.

1. Find two mixed numbers so that the sum is $8\frac{4}{8}$ and the difference is $2\frac{2}{8}$.

   _____

2. Find two mixed numbers so that the sum is $7\frac{2}{4}$ and the difference is 5.

   _____

3. Find two mixed numbers so that the sum is $7\frac{2}{8}$ and the difference is $2\frac{4}{8}$.

   _____

4. Find two mixed numbers so that the sum is $21\frac{1}{6}$ and the difference is $4\frac{3}{6}$.

   _____

5. Find two mixed numbers so that the sum is $15\frac{3}{10}$ and the difference is $8\frac{5}{10}$.

   _____

6. Find two mixed numbers so that the sum is 16 and the difference is 5.

   _____

7. **Stretch Your Thinking** Find three mixed numbers so that the sum is 18 and the difference between the greatest number and the least number is $5\frac{1}{5}$.

   _____

Enrich E60 Grade 4
© Houghton Mifflin Harcourt Publishing Company

Name _____

Lesson 7.8
Enrich

Leftovers

The fraction strips shown represent the whole number 33.
Subtract the numbers below from 33 by shading the
fraction strips. The fraction $\frac{3}{4}$ is shown as an example.

$\frac{3}{4}$ $3\frac{9}{16}$ $1\frac{7}{8}$ $2\frac{4}{5}$ $1\frac{7}{10}$ $\frac{5}{6}$ $1\frac{1}{3}$ $\frac{5}{12}$ $1\frac{3}{8}$ $1\frac{3}{5}$ $2\frac{1}{2}$ $1\frac{2}{3}$ $\frac{1}{6}$

$\frac{5}{16}$ $1\frac{3}{10}$ $\frac{5}{8}$ $\frac{7}{12}$ $1\frac{5}{6}$ $1\frac{2}{3}$ $\frac{3}{4}$ $1\frac{3}{5}$ $\frac{1}{3}$ $\frac{1}{6}$ $\frac{1}{10}$ $1\frac{9}{10}$ $\frac{1}{4}$

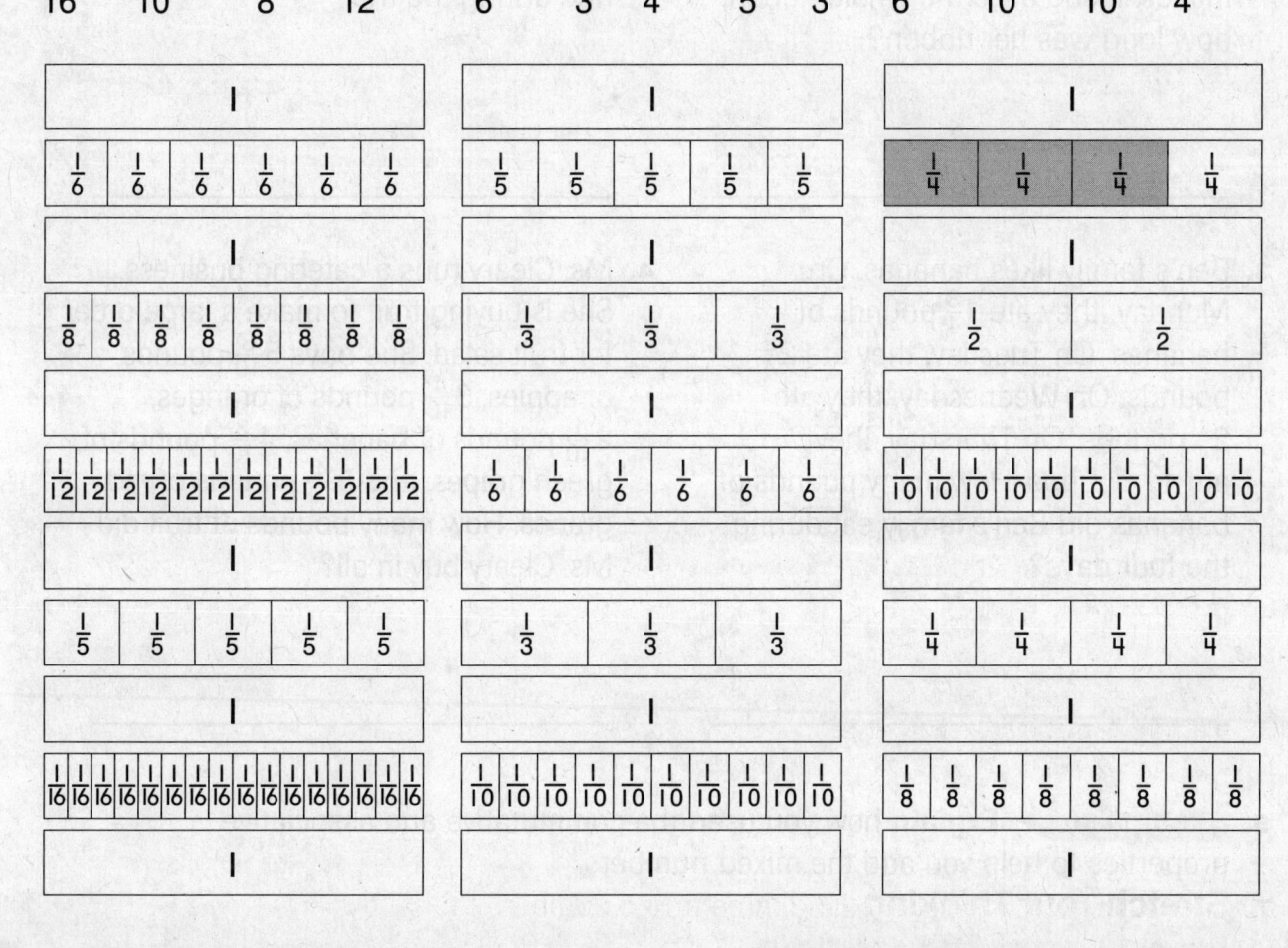

1. List the leftover fractions in the fraction strips.

   _____

2. What is the difference represented by the leftover fractions?

   _____

3. **Stretch Your Thinking** How can you model subtracting $\frac{1}{5}$ if you have only $\frac{1}{10}$ fraction strips?

   _____

   _____

   _____

Name _____

Lesson 7.9
Enrich

Mixing Properties

Use addition properties to help you solve each problem.

1. Robyn cut a length of ribbon into four pieces to wrap four gifts. The lengths she cut were $16\frac{7}{12}$ inches, $10\frac{3}{12}$ inches, $4\frac{9}{12}$ inches, and $10\frac{2}{12}$ inches. If she used the whole ribbon, how long was her ribbon?

   _____

2. Emily enjoys riding her bike. During a four-day biking trip, she rode $8\frac{1}{8}$ miles, $4\frac{3}{8}$ miles, $5\frac{4}{8}$ miles, $2\frac{7}{8}$ miles, and $6\frac{1}{8}$ miles. How many miles in all did she ride during the trip?

   _____

3. Ben's family likes bananas. On Monday, they ate $1\frac{3}{4}$ pounds of bananas. On Tuesday, they ate $2\frac{2}{4}$ pounds. On Wednesday, they ate $2\frac{1}{4}$ pounds. On Thursday, they ate $1\frac{2}{4}$ pounds. How many pounds of bananas did Ben's family eat during the four days?

   _____

4. Ms. Cleary runs a catering business. She is buying fruit to make a large order for fruit salad. She buys $5\frac{3}{10}$ pounds of apples, $3\frac{4}{10}$ pounds of oranges, $2\frac{1}{10}$ pounds of bananas, $4\frac{3}{10}$ pounds of green grapes, and $5\frac{4}{10}$ pounds of red grapes. How many pounds of fruit did Ms. Cleary buy in all?

   _____

5. **Write Math** ▸ **Explain** how you used the commutative and associative properties to help you add the mixed numbers.

   _____
   _____
   _____
   _____

Lesson 7.10
Enrich

Name _____

Problem Solving with Fractions

Solve each problem.

1. Cornelia cut equal lengths of ribbon each $\frac{7}{10}$ feet long. The ribbon was $3\frac{1}{2}$ feet long. How many pieces did Cornelia cut?

   _____

2. Tim walks $\frac{2}{3}$ mile to school each day. He walks the same distance home. How far does he walk to and from school during a regular school week (5 days)?

   _____

3. At a class pizza party, each pizza ordered had $\frac{2}{8}$ of the pizza left over after the party. In all, $1\frac{1}{2}$ pizzas were left over. How many pizzas were ordered?

   _____

4. A teacher had 10 pounds of raisins. He has 16 students. He gave each student $\frac{3}{5}$ pound. The teacher kept the leftover raisins for himself. How much did he keep for himself?

   _____

5. **Stretch Your Thinking** Explain how you solved Exercise 4.

   _____
   _____
   _____
   _____
   _____
   _____

Enrich

E63

Grade 4

© Houghton Mifflin Harcourt Publishing Company

Name _____

Lesson 8.1
Enrich

Mixed Numbers and Unit Fractions

Write each mixed number as the product of a whole number and a unit fraction.

1. $1\frac{1}{3}$

   _____

2. $3\frac{1}{2}$

   _____

3. $1\frac{3}{5}$

   _____

4. $2\frac{3}{8}$

   _____

5. $3\frac{3}{4}$

   _____

6. $5\frac{2}{3}$

   _____

7. $4\frac{2}{5}$

   _____

8. $5\frac{1}{5}$

   _____

9. **Write Math** ▶ **Explain** how you found the answer in Exercise 1.

_____
_____
_____
_____

Enrich   E64   Grade 4

Name _____

Lesson 8.2
Enrich

Multiples of Mixed Numbers

List the next three multiples of the mixed number. Write each multiple as a mixed number or as a whole number.

1. $1\frac{1}{8}$

   _____

2. $2\frac{1}{2}$

   _____

3. $1\frac{2}{3}$

   _____

4. $2\frac{1}{3}$

   _____

5. $3\frac{1}{5}$

   _____

6. $1\frac{1}{4}$

   _____

7. $1\frac{3}{5}$

   _____

8. $2\frac{3}{4}$

   _____

9. **Write Math** Describe a method other than multiplication that you can use to find the next three multiples of the mixed number in Exercise 7.

_____

_____

_____

_____

Enrich   E65   Grade 4
© Houghton Mifflin Harcourt Publishing Company

Name _____

Lesson 8.3
Enrich

Fraction of a Whole Number

Find the product. Write the product as a whole number.

1. $\frac{1}{8} \times 24 =$ _____

2. $\frac{2}{3} \times 15 =$ _____

3. $\frac{3}{5} \times 10 =$ _____

4. $\frac{4}{7} \times 14 =$ _____

5. $\frac{5}{6} \times 18 =$ _____

6. $\frac{3}{4} \times 16 =$ _____

7. $\frac{2}{9} \times 27 =$ _____

8. $\frac{7}{8} \times 32 =$ _____

9. $\frac{9}{10} \times 50 =$ _____

10. $\frac{4}{5} \times 45 =$ _____

11. $\frac{5}{12} \times 60 =$ _____

12. $\frac{8}{9} \times 54 =$ _____

13. **Write Math** Explain how you can tell if the product of a fraction and a whole number will be a whole number.

_____

_____

_____

Name _____

Lesson 8.4
Enrich

Unknown Numbers

Find the unknown number that makes each equation true.

1. $\blacksquare \times \dfrac{3}{4} = 2\dfrac{1}{4}$

2. $4 \times \dfrac{\blacksquare}{5} = 1\dfrac{3}{5}$

3. $7 \times \blacksquare = 1\dfrac{5}{9}$

4. $2 \times \blacksquare \dfrac{1}{3} = 6\dfrac{2}{3}$

5. $\blacksquare \times 1\dfrac{5}{6} = 9\dfrac{1}{6}$

6. $\blacksquare \times 2\dfrac{2}{7} = 13\dfrac{5}{7}$

7. **Write Math** ▶ **Explain** how you found the unknown number in Exercise 3.

Name _____

Lesson 8.5
Enrich

Heights and Depths

Solve each problem. You may find it helpful to draw a diagram.

1. The depth of Lake Carl is about $1\frac{1}{8}$ miles. Lake Susan is 3 times as deep as Lake Carl. Lake Wayne is 2 times as deep as Lake Susan. How much deeper is Lake Wayne than Lake Susan?

   _____

2. Mount Rogers rises $\frac{1}{4}$ mile above sea level. Mount Taylor rises 6 times as high as Mount Rogers. Mount Sullivan rises 2 times as high as Mount Rogers. What is the difference in the elevation of Mount Taylor and the elevation of Mount Sullivan?

   _____

3. A certain tree was $5\frac{1}{3}$ feet tall when it was first planted. A few years later, the tree is 4 times as tall as it was when it was first planted. How much has the tree grown since it was first planted?

   _____

4. **Write Math** ▶ **Explain** how you solved Problem 3.

   _____
   _____
   _____
   _____
   _____
   _____
   _____

Name _____

Lesson 9.1
Enrich

Model, Decimal, and Fraction

In each row of the table below, a model, a decimal, and a fraction or mixed number are shown for the same amount. Fill in the missing information.

Model	Decimal	Fraction or Mixed Number
1.	0.1	
2.		$2\frac{9}{10}$
3.	1.4	
4.		
5.		$3\frac{3}{10}$
6.		

7. In addition to the models used, in what other way could you represent the decimals, fractions, and mixed numbers?

_____

8. **Write Math** Describe how you filled in the missing model and fraction when only the decimal 1.4 was given.

_____
_____
_____

Enrich E69 Grade 4
© Houghton Mifflin Harcourt Publishing Company

Name _____

Lesson 9.2
Enrich

Which Hundredth Is It?

The number line below shows ten points, each labeled with a letter.

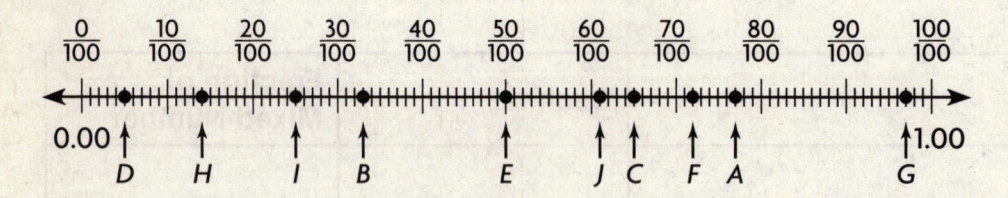

```
  0    10   20   30   40   50   60   70   80   90   100
 ───  ───  ───  ───  ───  ───  ───  ───  ───  ───  ───
 100  100  100  100  100  100  100  100  100  100  100
```

0.00 ↑   ↑   ↑   ↑   ↑   ↑ ↑   ↑   ↑1.00
      D   H   I   B   E   J C   F   G

For each fraction or decimal, write the letter that shows its position on the number line.

1. $\frac{65}{100}$ _____   6. 0.14 _____

2. $\frac{72}{100}$ _____   7. $\frac{5}{100}$ _____

3. 0.25 _____   8. 0.77 _____

4. $\frac{97}{100}$ _____   9. 0.61 _____

5. $\frac{33}{100}$ _____   10. 0.50 _____

11. Between which two letters would 0.75 be located? _____

12. **Write Math** Describe how you would order the ten fractions and decimals above from least to greatest.

_____

_____

_____

_____

Name _____

Lesson 9.3
Enrich

Matching Fractions and Decimals

Match each fraction or decimal in Column A with an equivalent fraction or decimal in Column B.

Column A	Column B
$\frac{2}{5}$	0.72
0.65	$\frac{1}{5}$
$\frac{18}{25}$	0.05
$\frac{9}{20}$	$\frac{3}{5}$
0.5	0.45
0.20	0.4
$\frac{3}{25}$	0.75
$\frac{3}{4}$	$\frac{13}{20}$
0.6	$\frac{1}{2}$
$\frac{1}{20}$	0.12

Write Math **Explain** how you found the match for $\frac{9}{20}$.

_____

_____

_____

_____

Enrich **E71** Grade 4

© Houghton Mifflin Harcourt Publishing Company

Name _____

Lesson 9.4
Enrich

Money Matters

For each fraction, write as a money amount and as a decimal in terms of dollars. Then write a combination of quarters, dimes, nickels, and pennies you could use to make that money amount.

1. $\frac{56}{100}$ _____   2. $\frac{75}{100}$ _____

3. $\frac{16}{100}$ _____   4. $\frac{5}{100}$ _____

5. $\frac{35}{100}$ _____   6. $\frac{70}{100}$ _____

7. $\frac{68}{100}$ _____   8. $\frac{99}{100}$ _____

9. $\frac{3}{100}$ _____   10. $\frac{33}{100}$ _____

11. Which fraction above can only be represented by one combination of coins? _____

12. **Write Math** Numbers that are represented as hundredths can sometimes also be represented as tenths. Use one of the fractions above to explain this possibility. Use money to support your answer.

_____

_____

Enrich   E72   Grade 4
© Houghton Mifflin Harcourt Publishing Company

Name _____

Lesson 9.5
Enrich

School Store

You are the cashier at the school store. Find how much change each customer should receive.

1. 1 notebook: $0.70
   1 pencil: $0.15

   The student pays with a $1 bill.

   _____

2. 1 pen: $0.75
   1 highlighter: $0.40
   1 eraser: $0.25

   The student pays with a $5 bill.

   _____

3. 2 notebooks: $0.85 each
   1 glue stick: $0.90
   1 sheet of stickers: $0.28

   The student pays with a $5 bill.

   _____

4. 1 writing tablet: $1.30
   3 pencils: $0.18 each
   2 pens: $1.07 each

   The student pays with a $10 bill.

   _____

5. **Write Math** **Explain** how you found the correct change for the customer in Exercise 3.

   _____

   _____

   _____

Enrich
© Houghton Mifflin Harcourt Publishing Company

E73

Grade 4

Name _____

Lesson 9.6
Enrich

Adding Fractions and Decimals

Use the trail information to find the distance each person hiked.

Trail Information
Nature Center to Eagle's Nest………0.8 miles
Eagle's Nest to Waterfall…………$\frac{53}{100}$ miles
Nature Center to Rickety Bridge……$\frac{6}{10}$ miles
Waterfall to Rickety Bridge………0.32 miles

1. Joni hiked from the Nature Center to Rickety Bridge and then from Rickety Bridge to the Waterfall.

2. Aaron hiked from the Nature Center to Eagle's Nest and then from Eagle's Nest to the Waterfall.

3. Iffat hiked from Eagle's Nest to the Waterfall, then to the Rickety Bridge, and then back to the Waterfall.

4. Troy hiked from the Nature Center to Eagle's Nest, then on to the Waterfall, from there to the Rickety Bridge, and then back to the Nature Center.

5. **Stretch Your Thinking** The Log Cabin is located near the Eagle's Nest, but it is not on the trail. It is a hike of 0.43 mile from Eagle's Nest. If the hiker in Exercise 4 also hiked to the Log Cabin and back to Eagle's Nest, how long would his total hike be?

Lesson 9.7
Enrich

Comparing Decimals

Solve each problem.

1. Abby ran the 50-yard dash in 7.05 seconds. Barb's time was 7.5 seconds. Chris's time was 6.94 seconds. List the runners in order from fastest to slowest.

_____
_____

2. Nick's bag weighs 5.4 kilograms. Amelia's bag weighs 2.26 kilograms. Nick's bag weighs 4.4 kilograms. List the weights of the bags from lightest to heaviest.

_____
_____

3. Jeremy has three lengths of string. One is 8.3 centimeters long. The second string is 8.32 centimeters long and the third string is 8.27 centimeters long. Order the lengths of Jeremy's strings from longest to shortest.

_____
_____

4. A science class is testing model planes. Group A's plane flew 9.35 meters. Group B's plane flew 9.6 meters. Group C's plane flew 10.04 meters. Group D's plane flew 9.57 meters. Which group's plane flew the shortest distance? the longest distance?

_____
_____

5. **Write Math** How do you compare decimals when the digits to the left of the decimal point are not 0?

_____
_____
_____
_____

Name _____

Lesson 10.1
Enrich

Line Art

Use geometric figures to draw each of the following.

1. A flower using 1 line segment and 8 rays.

2. A sidewalk using 2 lines and 6 line segments.

3. Use geometric figures to draw your own design. Choose from points, lines, rays, segments, and angles.

4. **Write Math** Describe your design in Problem 3. Include the names of the figures you chose.

_____
_____
_____
_____
_____
_____

Name _____

Lesson 10.2
Enrich

Triangle Living

In the space below, draw a living room design using only acute, right, and obtuse triangles. Then color the acute triangles one color, the right triangles a second color, and the obtuse triangles a third color.

Stretch Your Thinking How could you use the triangles to create rectangles and squares?

_____
_____
_____
_____

Name _____

Lesson 10.3
Enrich

Alphabet Soup

Use all 26 capital letters of the alphabet. Place them into as many "soups" as possible.

1. Letters with parallel line segments

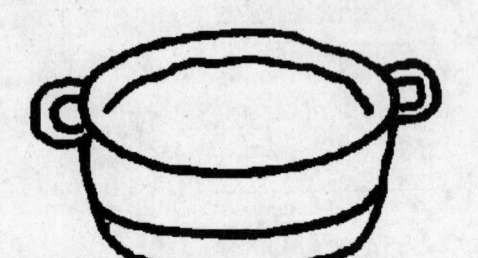

_____

2. Letters with perpendicular line segments

_____

3. Letters with intersecting, but not perpendicular, line segments

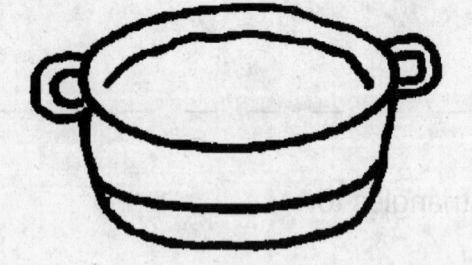

_____

4. Letters with no parallel, perpendicular, or intersecting line segments

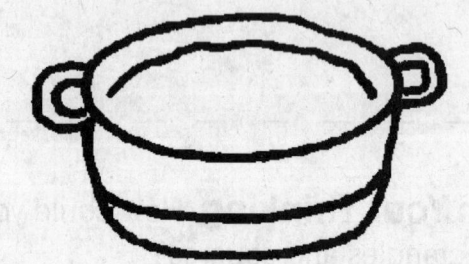

_____

Name _____

Lesson 10.4
Enrich

Quad Logic

Read each statement carefully. Write *true* or *false*.

1. Some parallelograms are rectangles. _____

2. All trapezoids are parallelograms. _____

3. All squares are rectangles. _____

4. Some quadrilaterals are trapezoids. _____

5. Some rectangles are rhombuses. _____

6. All rhombuses are squares. _____

7. Some parallelograms are trapezoids. _____

8. All rectangles are squares. _____

Make each statement true. Write *All, No,* or *Some*.

9. _____ rectangles are parallelograms.

10. _____ squares are trapezoids.

11. _____ parallelograms are quadrilaterals.

12. _____ quadrilaterals are parallelograms.

13. **Stretch Your Thinking** Write three of your own quad-logic statements. Then exchange them with a classmate and complete each other's statements.

_____

_____

Name _____

Lesson 10.5
Enrich

Swimming Pool Symmetry

The owner of the Seaside Symmetry Resort is designing a new swimming pool. The owner wants the pool to have line symmetry. Tell if each swimming pool design below appears to have line symmetry. If it does, draw a line or lines of symmetry.

1.

2.

3.

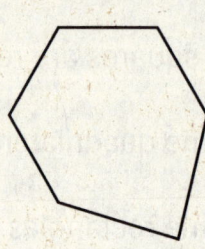

_____   _____   _____

4.

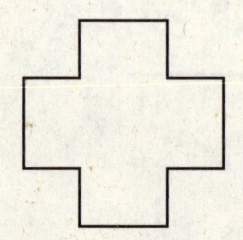

5.

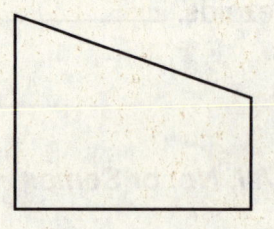

6.

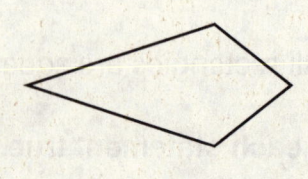

_____   _____   _____

7. The owner of the resort wants to build a pool that has four sides with equal length and four lines of symmetry. In what shape can the pool be built?

_____

8. **Write Math** ▶ Describe a strategy you could use to make a symmetrical design for a swimming pool.

_____
_____
_____
_____

Enrich

E80

Grade 4

© Houghton Mifflin Harcourt Publishing Company

Name _____

Lesson 10.6
Enrich

Symmetry Riddle

What did the 0 say to the 8?

To answer the riddle, use the decoding box for each word. For each shape, decide how many lines of symmetry it appears to have, and then use the code. For example, a square has 4 lines of symmetry, so write an N on the line below the square.

1. Word 1 Code Box

Write C if the shape has no lines of symmetry.
Write E if the shape has 1 line of symmetry.
Write F if the shape has 2 lines of symmetry.
Write I if the shape has 3 lines of symmetry.
Write N if the shape has 4 lines of symmetry.
Write R if the shape has 6 lines of symmetry.

Word 1

N ___ ___ ___

2. Word 2 Code Box

Write B if the shape has no lines of symmetry.
Write E if the shape has 1 line of symmetry.
Write G if the shape has 2 lines of symmetry.
Write L if the shape has 3 lines of symmetry.
Write O if the shape has 4 lines of symmetry.
Write T if the shape has 6 lines of symmetry.

Word 2

___ ___ ___ ___

3. **Write Math** ▸ Make up your own symmetry riddle and code boxes. Exchange riddles with your classmates and solve.

_____

_____

_____

_____

Name _____

Lesson 10.7
Enrich

Pentomino Patterns

A *pentomino* is a figure made of five same-size squares. Each square must share a side with its neighbor.

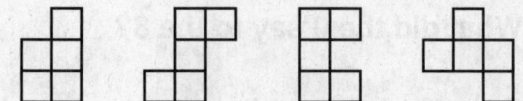

The pattern at the right uses two pentominoes to create a rectangular design.

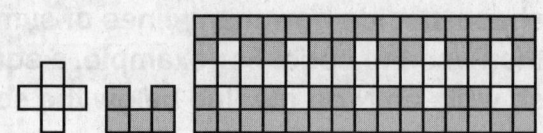

Use the pentominoes to create a rectangular design.

1.

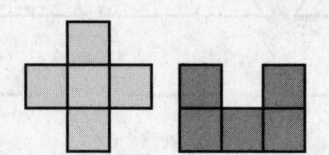

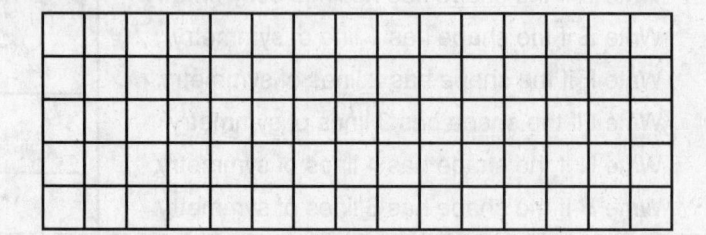

2.

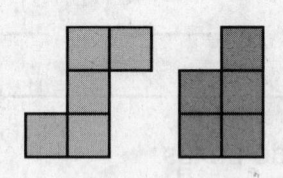

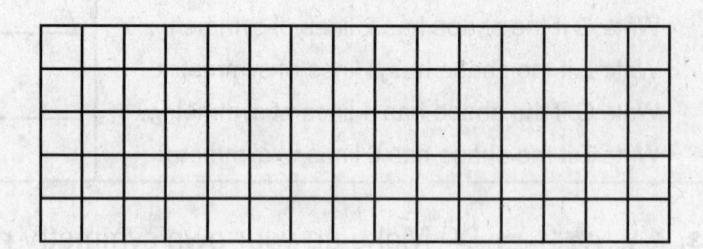

3.

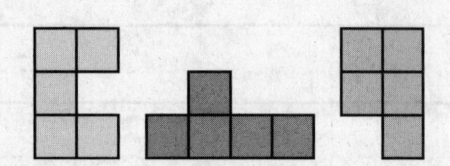

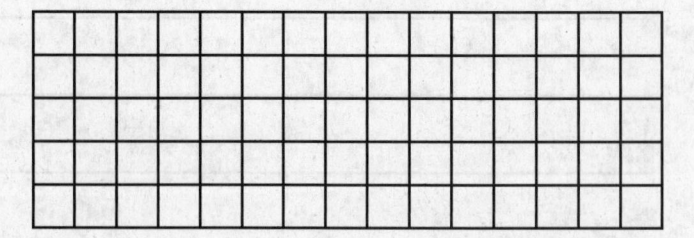

Enrich E82 Grade 4
© Houghton Mifflin Harcourt Publishing Company

Name _____

Lesson 11.1
Enrich

A Turning Riddle

What is the best way to eat soup?

Use the circle below. For each exercise, start at the top of the circle, make the indicated turn, and write the letter on the blank line. When you have finished, read the letters from top to bottom to answer the riddle.

1. $\frac{1}{12}$ turn counterclockwise _____
2. $\frac{5}{12}$ turn clockwise _____
3. $\frac{1}{6}$ turn counterclockwise _____
4. $\frac{1}{3}$ turn clockwise _____
5. $\frac{1}{12}$ turn clockwise _____
6. $\frac{1}{4}$ turn counterclockwise _____
7. $\frac{8}{12}$ turn clockwise _____
8. $\frac{7}{12}$ turn clockwise _____
9. $\frac{5}{12}$ turn counterclockwise _____
10. $\frac{1}{2}$ turn counterclockwise _____

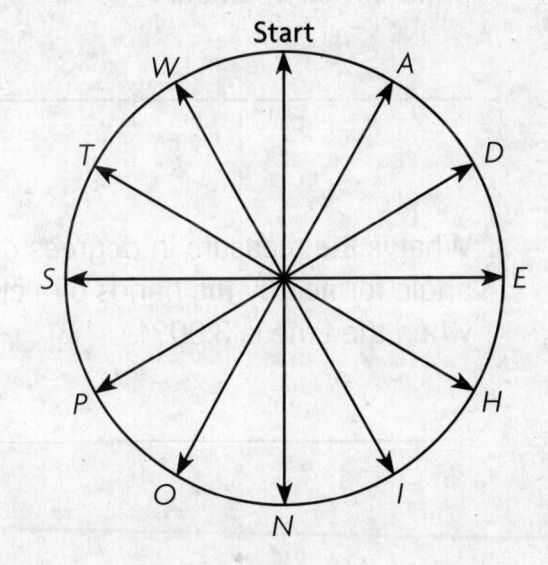

11. **Write Math** ▸ Make up your own riddle and answer circle. Exchange it with a classmate and solve.

_____
_____
_____

Enrich   E83   Grade 4
© Houghton Mifflin Harcourt Publishing Company

Name _____

Lesson 11.2
Enrich

Time by Degrees

Use the hands of a clock to answer each question.

1. How many degrees does the minute hand turn to get from 12:00 to 12:05?

   _____

2. How many degrees does the minute hand turn to get from 12:00 to 12:20?

   _____

3. How many degrees does the hour hand turn in one hour?

   _____

4. How many degrees does the hour hand turn to get from 12:00 to 12:20?

   _____

5. What is the measure in degrees of the angle formed by the hands of a clock when the time is 3:00?

   _____

6. What is the degree measure of the angle formed by the hands of a clock when the time is 12:00?

   _____

7. What is the degree measure of the angle formed by the hands of a clock when the time is 9:00?

   _____

8. What is the measure in degrees of the angle formed by the hands of a clock when the time is 6:00?

   _____

9. **Stretch Your Thinking** What is the degree measure of the angle formed by the hands of a clock when the time is 3:30?

   _____

Enrich

E84

Grade 4

© Houghton Mifflin Harcourt Publishing Company

Name _____

Lesson 11.3
Enrich

Drawing Triangles

For Exercises 1–4, draw and label a triangle with the given angle measures.

1. 60°, 60°, 60°

2. 90°, 35°, 55°

3. 42°, 64°, 74°

4. 118°, 31°, 31°

5. **Stretch Your Thinking** Compare your triangles with those of several classmates. What do you notice?

_____

_____

_____

Name _____

Lesson 11.4
Enrich

Degrees of Separation

Use a protractor. For each exercise, measure and label the angle.
Then separate the angle as instructed and label the measures of its parts.

1. Separate the angle into two equal angles.

2. Separate the angle into three equal angles.

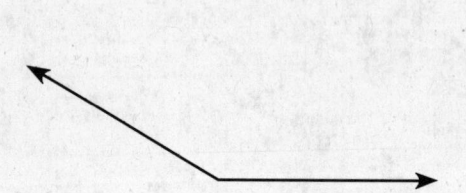

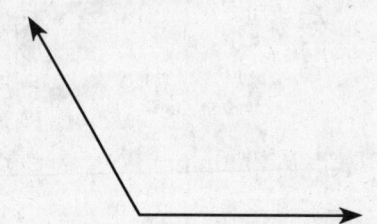

3. Separate the angle into two angles such that one angle is 15° greater than the other.

4. Separate the angle into three angles such that the greatest angle is 2 times as large as the smallest angle. The greatest angle also measures 20° more than the third angle.

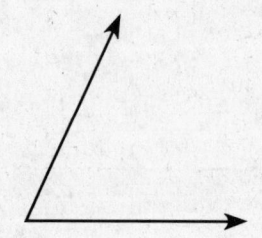

5. **Write Math** Describe how you used a protractor to complete the exercises.

_____

_____

_____

Enrich　　　　　　　　　　E86　　　　　　　　　　Grade 4

Name _____

Lesson 11.5
Enrich

Unknown Measures

In Exercises 1–4, three angles join to form a straight angle.
Use the information given to find the measure of each angle.

1. One angle is a right angle. Give three pairs of possible measures for the other two angles.

   _____

   _____

   _____

2. One angle measures 40°. The other two angles have the same measure. What is the measure of each angle?

   _____

3. All three angles have the same measure. What is the measure of each angle?

   _____

4. One angle measures 30°. The measure of the second angle is 2 times as large as the measure of the third angle. What are the measures of the other two angles?

   _____

5. **Stretch Your Thinking** Draw any two triangles and measure the angles in each. Find the sum of the angle measures. Look back at the angle measures you found in Exercises 1–4. Can you draw a triangle for each set? **Explain.**

   _____

   _____

   _____

Name _____

Lesson 12.1
Enrich

Estimation Match-Up

Match each sentence on the left with an appropriate unit on the right.

1. The weight of Tom's pick-up truck is more than one _____.

   centimeter

2. A cat's tail has a length that is more than one _____.

   gallon

3. A milk carton holds more than one _____ of milk.

   ton

4. A crayon is less than one _____ long.

   meter

5. A water balloon is filled with less than one _____ of water.

   mile

6. A paper clip weighs less than one _____.

   fluid ounce

7. Tina's puppy weighs more than one _____.

   pound

8. A marathon runner jogged more than one _____.

   ounce

9. **Stretch Your Thinking** Suppose two objects are the same size. Must they weigh the same amount? Give an example to explain.

_____

_____

_____

Enrich
© Houghton Mifflin Harcourt Publishing Company

Name _____

Lesson 12.2
Enrich

Inching Closer

Solve each problem.

1. In a football game, a running back gained $4\frac{1}{2}$ yards on one play. What is this distance in inches?

   _____

2. Margie is $5\frac{1}{3}$ feet tall. How many inches tall is she?

   _____

3. A quarterback threw a football 10 yards 2 feet 1 inch. How many inches did the quarterback throw the football?

   _____

4. From a standing position, Meg jumps 7 feet 4 inches and Victor jumps 9 feet 2 inches. How many inches farther does Victor jump than Meg?

   _____

5. Jeremy ran 5 yards 2 feet 3 inches. In the same time, John ran 9 yards 1 foot 10 inches. How many inches farther did John run than Jeremy?

   _____

6. A rectangular flower garden measures 3 yards 1 foot 8 inches wide and 1 yard 2 feet 3 inches long. How many inches of fencing is needed to enclose the entire flower garden?

   _____

7. **Write Math** **Explain** how you solved Problem 6.

_____

_____

_____

_____

Name _____

Lesson 12.3
Enrich

Weighty Matters

Solve each problem.

1. A truck weighs 1 ton 1,350 pounds. The weight limit for a bridge is given in pounds. How many pounds does the truck weigh?

   _____

2. Jasmine's new kitten weighs 2 pounds 6 ounces. Feeding instructions are given for weights in ounces. How many ounces does the kitten weigh?

   _____

3. At the zoo, one elephant weighs 7 tons 400 pounds. Another elephant weighs 4 tons 1,800 pounds. How many more pounds does the first elephant weigh?

   _____

4. Jim's dog weighs 18 pounds 10 ounces. His cat weighs 6 pounds 3 ounces. How many more ounces does Jim's dog weigh than his cat?

   _____

5. Owen's math book weighs 2 pounds 13 ounces. His science book weighs 1 pound 15 ounces. His backpack weighs 1 pound 1 ounce. What is the total weight in ounces of the backpack and the two books?

   _____

6. A truck is transporting 6 cars to a dealership. Each car weighs 1 ton 1,400 pounds. What is the total weight in pounds of the cars the truck is transporting?

   _____

7. **Write Math** **Explain** how you solved Problem 3.

   _____
   _____
   _____
   _____

Enrich   E90   Grade 4

© Houghton Mifflin Harcourt Publishing Company

Lesson 12.4
Enrich

Name _____

Using Measures of Liquid Volume

Solve each problem.

1. At his lemonade stand, Ishmael has enough lemonade mix to make 3 gallons 2 quarts 1 pint of lemonade. How many 1-cup servings of lemonade can he make?

   _____

2. Irene has 1 gallon of milk. She uses 4 fluid ounces of milk in each bowl of cereal. How many bowls of cereal can she fill before she has used all the milk?

   _____

3. One day at lunch, the cafeteria sold thirty-four 1-pint containers of milk. The cafeteria also sold forty-eight 12-fl-oz bottles of water. Did the cafeteria sell more fluid ounces of water or milk? How many more?

   _____

4. Mrs. Nelson bought a 2-gallon container of ice cream. How many 2-fl-oz scoops of ice cream can be served from this container?

   _____

5. **Write Math** **Explain** how you solved Problem 3.

   _____

   _____

   _____

   _____

Enrich　　　　　　　　　　　　　　　E91　　　　　　　　　　　　　　　Grade 4

Name _____

Lesson 12.5
Enrich

Discover the Line Plot

The students in Richie's class were asked how much juice they drink at breakfast. Use the clues to make a line plot. Draw your line plot in the space below. Remember to include a title.

1.	The most any student drinks is $1\frac{1}{2}$ cups of juice.
2.	The response given most often was $\frac{3}{4}$ cup. The number of responses was 1 more than the next greatest amount.
3.	Two students said that they don't drink any juice in the morning.
4.	The students drink a total of $8\frac{1}{4}$ cups of juice.
5.	Three students drink 1 cup of juice each.
6.	Together, only three students gave a response of $\frac{1}{4}$, $\frac{1}{2}$, $1\frac{1}{4}$, or $1\frac{1}{2}$; and none of these had more than 1 response.

Cups of Juice Students Drink at Breakfast

```
                    X
                    X
                    X
X                   X
X         X         X         X
X    X    X    X    X         X
―――――――――――――――――――――――――――――――
0   1/4  1/2  3/4   1   1 1/4  1 1/2
```

7. **Stretch Your Thinking** What fraction of the students drank more than $\frac{1}{2}$ cup of juice? **Explain.**

_____

_____

_____

Name _____

Lesson 12.6
Enrich

Going to Greater Lengths

The kilometer is a metric unit of length that is equal to 1,000 meters. Use this information and what you already know about metric length to answer the questions.

1. Edward entered into a 5-kilometer race. How many meters will he need to run?

   _____

2. Nancy walked 2 kilometers from her house to the library. How many decimeters did she walk?

   _____

3. Jed rode his bike 1.5 kilometers from home to school. How many centimeters did Jed ride?

   _____

4. Ursula hiked $6\frac{1}{2}$ kilometers through the woods. How many decimeters did she hike?

   _____

5. An Olympic swimming pool is 50 meters long. How many lengths would Ian have to swim in order to swim 1 kilometer?

   _____

6. Terence ran 3 kilometers in the same time it took Ali to run 2,400 meters. Who ran farther? How much farther?

   _____

7. **Stretch Your Thinking** The **hectometer** is another metric unit of length. 1 hectometer = 100 meters. What is the relationship between kilometers and hectometers?

   _____

Enrich

E93

Grade 4

© Houghton Mifflin Harcourt Publishing Company

Name _____

Lesson 12.7
Enrich

More Volume, Less Mass

The milligram is a metric unit of mass. One gram is equal to 1,000 milligrams. The kiloliter is a unit of metric volume that is equal to 1,000 liters. Use this information and what you know about metric units to answer the questions.

1. A small swimming pool contains 6 kiloliters of water. How many liters of water does the pool contain?

   _____

2. A scientist has a 3-gram sample of soil to analyze. How many milligrams is the soil sample?

   _____

3. About 1 kiloliter of water runs past a certain point in a freshwater stream each minute. How many 2-liter bottles could be filled from 1 kiloliter of water?

   _____

4. A pill contains 200 milligrams of medicine. If Barb takes one pill each day, how many grams of medicine does she take in 10 days?

   _____

5. Helen places a 2-gram mass on one side of a scale. How many milligrams would it take to balance the scale?

   _____

6. A storage tank holds 4 kiloliters of water. How many liters of water does the tank hold?

   _____

7. **Write Math** ▶ **Explain** how you found the answer to Problem 4.

   _____
   _____
   _____

Enrich   E94   Grade 4
© Houghton Mifflin Harcourt Publishing Company

Name _____

Lesson 12.8
Enrich

Passing the Time

Solve each problem.

1. Barry left his flashlight on. The batteries lost power after 2 weeks 5 days 15 hours. How many hours was it before the flashlight lost power?

2. A rocket launch is scheduled to take place in 3 weeks 4 days 22 hours. How many hours is it until the rocket is launched?

3. In October 2010, the winning time in the men's division of the Chicago Marathon was 2 hours 6 minutes 24 seconds. How many seconds did it take the winner to run the marathon?

4. Patti and her friends want to see one of two movies. One movie starts in 1 day 2 hours 20 minutes. The other movie starts in 1 day 4 hours 10 minutes. The later movie starts at 5:00 P.M. At what time does the earlier movie start?

5. **Write Math** ▸ **Explain** how you solved Problem 1.

Name _____

Lesson 12.9
Enrich

Do You Have the Time?

Read each problem to find the time.

1. Jordan needs to leave for school at 8:15 A.M. It takes her 20 minutes total to get dressed and brush her teeth, and 15 minutes to eat breakfast. What time does she need to wake up?

   _____

2. Louis starts walking at 4:30 P.M. He walks for 35 minutes before stopping for a snack. He takes 15 minutes to eat his snack. At what time will he start walking again?

   _____

3. Trevor spent 15 minutes in the shoe store, 25 minutes in the candle store, and then 10 minutes in the card store. Trevor left the card store at 10:45 A.M. What time did he arrive at the shoe store?

   _____

4. Soccer practice begins at 5:30 P.M. The team spends the first 15 minutes doing stretches, and then the next 10 minutes doing dribbling drills. If the coach gives a 5-minute water break before the next activity, what time will that activity start?

   _____

5. Betsy finished her math and science homework at 4:25 P.M. If she took 15 minutes to complete her math homework and 20 minutes to complete her science homework, what time did she start?

   _____

6. **Write Math** Describe the steps you took to solve Problem 4.

   _____
   _____
   _____

Lesson 12.10
Enrich

Name _____

Mixed Measures

Solve each problem.

1. Ted's new puppy weighed 8 pounds 11 ounces two months ago. One month later, the puppy had gained 2 pounds 7 ounces. During the second month, the puppy gained 3 pounds 5 ounces. How much does Ted's puppy weigh now?

   _____

2. Gilda made 2 gallons of lemonade to sell at her lemonade stand. At the end of the day, she had 2 quarts 1 pint left over. How many 1-cup servings did Gilda sell?

   _____

3. Four friends competed in a relay race. Each friend ran one leg of the race. Ann ran her leg in 2 minutes 15 seconds. Kyra ran her leg in 1 minute 53 seconds. Marie ran her leg in 2 minutes 9 seconds. Zoe ran the final leg in 1 minute 58 seconds. What was the total time for the relay team?

   _____

4. Ron timed his flight from Los Angeles to New York. The plane was in the air for 4 hours 52 minutes 45 seconds. The return trip took longer because of a headwind. Ron recorded the flight time as 5 hours 34 minutes 14 seconds. How much longer was the return flight?

   _____

5. **Write Math** ▶ **Explain** how you converted units to solve Problem 2.

   _____
   _____
   _____
   _____
   _____

Enrich   E97   Grade 4
© Houghton Mifflin Harcourt Publishing Company

Name _____

Lesson 12.11
Enrich

Two-Step Patterns

Use unit relationships and write a pattern to solve each problem.

1. Jessie hops for 1 minute then rests for 15 seconds. She repeats this pattern for several minutes. Write a pattern showing the number of seconds when Jessie switches from one activity to the next. After how many seconds will she start resting for the fourth time?

   _____

2. A snail creeps up a plank 8 centimeters each day and slides back down 15 millimeters each night. Write a numerical pattern showing the number of millimeters where the snail changes direction. On which day will the snail have moved 275 millimeters up from its starting point?

   _____

3. Joel is doing an experiment. He adds 2 gallons of water to a large tub each week. During the week, 1 quart 1 cup of water evaporates. Write a numerical pattern showing the number of cups of water before and after Joel adds water. How long will it take until there are more than 100 cups of water in the tub?

   _____

4. **Stretch Your Thinking** In Problem 2, after how many days will the snail be 65 centimeters ahead? **Explain.**

   _____

   _____

   _____

Name _____

Lesson 13.1
Enrich

Perimeter Puzzlers

1. The shaded rectangle has a perimeter of 18 cm. Draw a different rectangle that has a perimeter of 18 cm.

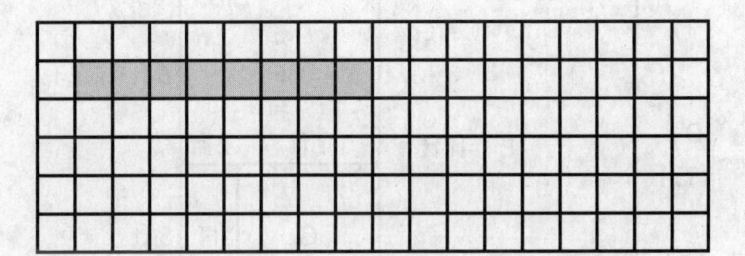

2. Draw a square and find the perimeter. Then draw a rectangle that has the same perimeter as the square.

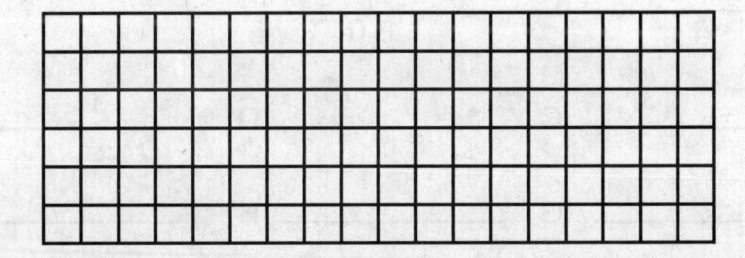

Find the unknown length for each rectangle.

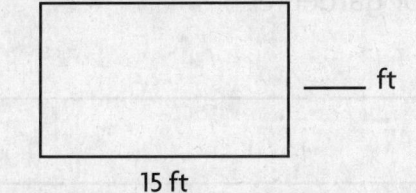

3. ____ ft

15 ft

Perimeter = 50 ft

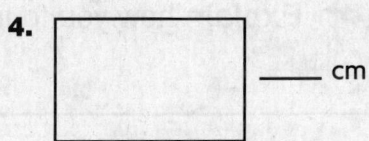

4. ____ cm

30 cm

Perimeter = 96 cm

Enrich E99 Grade 4

Name _____

Lesson 13.2
Enrich

Aiden's Garden

Find the area of each rectangular garden using the formula $A = b \times h$.
Write your answer for each garden on the line provided.

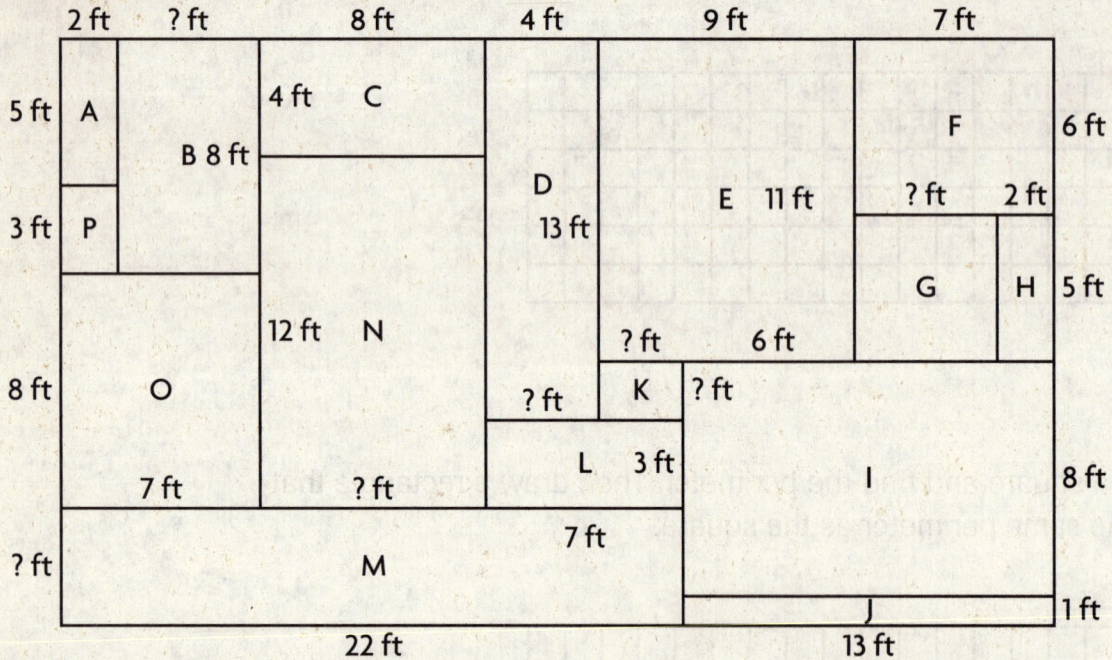

1.

A _____ B _____ C _____ D _____

E _____ F _____ G _____ H _____

I _____ J _____ K _____ L _____

M _____ N _____ O _____ P _____

2. **Write Math** ▶ **Explain** how you found the area for garden G.

_____

_____

_____

_____

Lesson 13.3
Enrich

Unusual Measures

A very long time ago, people used body units to measure lengths.

Span   length from the end of the thumb to the end of the little finger when hand is stretched fully

Cubit   length from the elbow to the end of the longest finger

Fathom   length from fingertip to fingertip when arms are stretched fully in opposite directions

You can use body measures to estimate the areas of objects at school. List some objects. Then choose the most appropriate unit to estimate the area of the object. Record your results in the chart below. Follow the two examples shown.

Object Measured	Measured in Spans Area	Measured in Cubits Area	Measured in Fathoms Area
Desk Top	12 square spans	2 square cubits	
1.			
2.			
3.			
4.			

5. **Write Math**   **Explain** how you found the area in square spans.

_____

_____

_____

_____

Enrich   E101   Grade 4
© Houghton Mifflin Harcourt Publishing Company

Name _____

Lesson 13.4
Enrich

Rectangular Riddles

Solve each riddle.

1. I am a rectangle. My perimeter is 60 feet. My length is twice as long as my width. How much area do I cover?

   _____

2. I am a rectangle, and my area is 80 square inches. My width is 2 inches shorter than my length. What is my perimeter?

   _____

3. I am the fencing around the rectangular lion exhibit at a zoo. The lions have 1,000 square meters to roam inside a rectangular area that is 15 meters longer than it is wide. If I were to unwind and make myself straight, how long would I be?

   _____

4. I am a rectangular picture frame. If I were straight, I would be 120 inches long. I am wrapped around a picture, and my length is twice as long as my width. What is the area of the picture that I am wrapped around?

   _____

5. **Stretch Your Thinking** Write two of your own rectangular riddles. Write one that asks for perimeter and one that asks for area.

   _____

   _____

   _____

   _____

   _____

   _____

Enrich   E102   Grade 4
© Houghton Mifflin Harcourt Publishing Company

Name _____

Lesson 13.5
Enrich

Building Bedrooms

The Harrisons have two children. They need your help with designing a bedroom for each child. Here are the conditions.

- Both rooms must be rectangular and have one wall in common.
- All measurements must be in whole feet.
- The walls are 8 feet high.
- Each room must have a door and at least two windows.
- Up to 100 feet of border in total may be used for the walls of the two rooms.

In the space below, design the two bedrooms for the Harrisons. Label all dimensions.

1. How much carpeting will be needed to cover the floors of both rooms?

   _____

2. One can of paint covers 200 square feet. Estimate how many cans of paint will be needed to paint the walls of both rooms.

   _____

Enrich   E103   Grade 4